IN DYLAN TOWN

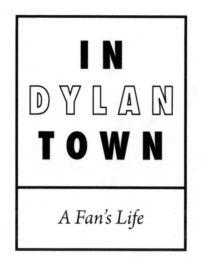

IN DYLAN TOWN

A Fan's Life

DAVID GAINES

University of Iowa Press, Iowa City

University of Iowa Press, Iowa City 52242
Copyright © 2015 by the University of Iowa Press
www.uiowapress.org
Printed in the United States of America

Design by Ashley Muehlbauer

The University of Iowa Press is a member of Green
Press Initiative and is committed to preserving natural
resources.

Printed on acid-free paper

Library of Congress Cataloging-in-Publication Data
Gaines, David, 1950–author.
In Dylan town : a fan's life / David Gaines.
pages cm
Includes bibliographical references and index.
ISBN 978-1-60938-363-3 (pbk)
ISBN 978-1-60938-364-0 (ebk)
1. Dylan, Bob, 1941—Influence.
2. Fans (Persons)   I. Title.
ML420.D98G35   2015
782.42164092—dc23   2015005543

For

my families, and

most of all for

Norma, Buddy, Kell, Rach, and Sid

"Sure as the world ..."

Someday, everything is gonna be smooth like a rhapsody . . .
—Bob Dylan, "When I Paint My Masterpiece"

CONTENTS

PREFACE

It was the first week of October 2009, the sun was setting, and my wife, Norma, and I were at a bar called the Kettle of Fish, fifteen minutes early for the monthly New York City Dylan meet-up. We were in from the provinces, wearing our new scarves, and having a moment in Lower Manhattan. We had just walked through the West Village on Christopher Street. "Sort of like Dylan in early 1961," I told Norma, invoking the kind of historically rich, even if not exactly spot-on, information those of us who pride ourselves on knowing our Dylan like to fold into our daily lives. Norma, having heard more than her fair share of Dylan references over the years, nodded, smiled her Mona Lisa smile, and said, "Exactly" because, as Dylan put it in "Love Minus Zero, No Limit," *she knows too much to argue or to judge.*

We had come to town as guest speakers for a class on "Bob Dylan's Art and Life" at the 92nd Street Y, the cultural institution where, in the 904-seat Kaufmann Concert Hall, several of our literary heroes had read and performed. In a small classroom on the third floor, I would be talking about Dylan's senses of humor and Norma would discuss his paintings in *The Drawn Blank Series* (2008). There were no ads in *The New Yorker* or *The Village Voice* about our event. But we were only a few floors above the concert hall and that was heady enough stuff for me.

Nina Goss, the course's instructor and editor of the Dylan fanzine *Montague Street*, had invited us. We had met Nina two years earlier when I spoke about Dylan's song "Chimes of Freedom" to Bob Levinson's New School class. For years Levinson offered a course that brought in people who worked with, wrote about, or taught classes based on Dylan to talk with students interested in Dylan. He had created an epicenter for Dylan fans of many stripes and, in so doing, encouraged those fans to share their responses to Dylan's fifty years of writing and performing everything from talking blues to finger-pointing songs to rock and roll about the complexities of love. Fully aware that I was using my armchair anthropological vocabulary very loosely, I would tell anyone willing to listen, "Levinson enlarged our tribe."

During the day Levinson worked in his family's home furnishing business. On the weekends, he had a radio show on Long Island devoted to Dylan, a program in which he spoke in a deep, New York, holy-man-on-the-FM-radio voice. He was a large, thick-mustached guy who talked fast and, as I learned when I came to the city, walked even faster. Most importantly to me, he knew and loved everything about Dylan. He rhapsodized about how the harmonica solo in "Mr. Tambourine Man" changed his life, told stories of growing up in and around the Village in the Sixties, and took pilgrim fans on tours of Dylan's old haunts. Such fans knew these haunts from the photographs and biographies and memoirs, just as fans cut from different cloths knew their Civil War battlefields or Dickens's London or Elvis's Memphis. Levinson was a long-standing and deep Dylan fan with some serious New York access. He referred to Dylan as *Bob*, never implying that he knew him personally but rather that he was connected to him spiritually. It was all in the inflection, and those who knew their Dylan—the real fans—totally got it.

Levinson had come across a quote that I had given a journalist about Dylan's *Theme Time Radio Hour*, a satellite radio program on which Dylan selected and talked about his favorite music. Each week he organized his musical selections and commentary around a different theme. Baseball, weather, flowers, the Bible, friends and neighbors, coffee, Texas, tears, laughter, time, marriage, and divorce were but a few of the big tents under which he pitched individual episodes. Levinson told me he liked what I had said about Dylan being an omnivorous pop musicologist with a quirky sense of humor. E-mails were exchanged, stories about our families and the New York Giants were shared, and I was invited to speak at the New School, where Nina was a student in Levinson's class. A few years later Levinson passed the teaching torch to Nina. A few more pages flew off the calendar, a few more stars aligned, and Norma and I found ourselves in the Kettle of Fish, waiting for the meet-up.

Nina had told us that the night before our presentations a few people were getting together, as they did every month, to talk about Dylan. "Ron Rosenbaum might be coming. He's working on a book about Dylan and religion," Nina had told me over the phone. "Levinson probably won't be there. We'll meet at the Kettle." I knew that our hero, a few months shy of his twentieth birthday and just arrived from Hibbing, Minnesota, in 1961, had hung out at the Kettle when it was on MacDougal Street. The landmark had moved a few blocks and become a bar with Green Bay Packers décor. It was wood-paneled and had Christmas lights that were probably on year-round. Even though it wasn't the original thing, I could still close my eyes and imagine Dylan and his friends there, as he put it in

"Bob Dylan's Dream," *laughin' and singin' till the early hours of the morn.* I opened my eyes, ordered from the barmaid in the Aaron Rodgers jersey, and waited.

Nina and her husband, Charlie, arrived, as did two of their Dylan friends. They took off their coats and scarves. I'd forgotten how petite Nina is and how much her hair reminded me of Dylan's during his *Blonde on Blonde* days. Just as John Lennon started to resemble Yoko the longer they were together, Nina was looking ever more like Bob the more she immersed herself in his art. To describe Nina's interest in and playfulness with Dylan's work as immersion is to understate the case greatly. She brought such wide-ranging intelligence and intense passion to the undertaking that I found myself racing to keep up with her. Her generous response to my presentation about "Chimes of Freedom"—her comments in prose that connected the political, personal, and aesthetic—had been our second time of comparing Dylan notes. This evening would be our third. Charlie was in his mid- to late-forties, soft-spoken, gracious, and as passionate about Dylan as Nina was. Walter might have been fifteen years older and was the chair of the English Department at Pace University. Brian, I guessed, was thirty-something, but looked just out of college. No one would mistake us for musicians or Green Bay Packers. Nods of recognition were exchanged, Brian's a bit more animated than anyone else's, and the meet-up came to order.

Before they even got their drinks or we made small talk about what we did in our non-Dylan lives, Walter casually asked, "David, what's the first track on *Street Legal*?" This question about one of Dylan's less-discussed albums was not as unnerving as any question that the not-yet-there Rosenbaum, one of my journalistic idols, might have asked. But, as an icebreaker, it did take me aback. It was gently asked and, at the same time, well designed to plumb the depths of my knowledge and commitment. I was immediately in the thick of it, racing through my database as quickly as possible, all the while trying not to tip my increasingly frantic hand and reveal that I might indeed fail my initial, and thereby only, test of the evening. I took a sip of my Rolling Rock, swallowed, and said, "I know this."

I was stalling for time. Except for the beer, it was a lot like being back in grade school in the Fifties and trying to get through those pesky multiplication tables. Or, scarier yet, as my mind shifted into third gear, I flashed back to my doctoral defense in 1980 when dissertation committee member Bob Crunden, who prided himself on being no great fan of any music after Virgil Thomson, asked me, "Why should we care about popular culture, Mr. Gaines? Really, why?"

Sipping once more and shaking just a little, I shifted into fourth gear: Street Legal! *Dylan in doorway with jacket, gray pants, white shoes, waiting on a friend. First track? Too late for "Hurricane." "New Pony"? Too early for "Gotta Serve Somebody." Why not a question about* Blood on the Tracks? *Will Rosenbaum show up? Is Brian tapping his foot because everyone who is anyone knows the first track? Or is he just a foot tapper?* Three seconds had passed, and I could feel the muscles in my shoulders tightening and my pulse quickening as my adrenaline approached the top of that first roller-coaster incline.

Walter filled the void and was just about to move us along. "Not to worry. That's a tough one," he said as he looked around the table with an expression that was probably about beverages, although I thought I detected the slightest bit of disappointment that I had not lived up to whatever qualifications my Dylan-teaching credentials suggested. We were, I felt certain, on the verge of a civilized beer, maybe even two, but no real connection. There would be none of that magical, nonstop witty, Algonquin Round Table give-and-take of those legendary *New Yorker* days that I had been imagining ever since Nina had invited us. Thank God that Rosenbaum wasn't there to witness this. Too bad that Norma, Nina, and Charlie were.

Then, out of nowhere, almost a full ten seconds after Walter had asked his question, with one of my feet in the meet-up grave and my other one heading that way, one of those angels that lands on my shoulder every few decades turned me into its ventriloquist dummy and I blurted out, "Changing of the Guards." Even more adrenaline, the stuff of that first big dip down the roller-coaster track or that moment when your fingertips first break the icy water you are diving into, shot through me. Somehow, by way of Dylan, I had once again learned that I knew something I didn't think I knew. I was going to be able to keep up with the gang.

No one high-fived or cheered me. That would have been very un-Bob. After all, we weren't playing a round of Trivial Pursuit or at a *Star Trek* convention. Nor were we sports fans trading ESPN minutiae. No, we were Dylan people who would never use a word like "Dylanologist" to describe ourselves, as the mainstream media tended to do. We were early- to late-middle-aged fans comparing opinions about our favorite albums, songs, performances, and best guesses regarding the next leg of Dylan's Never-Ending Tour. We knew the code, cared about the same kinds of open-ended questions, and shared Dylan as our desert island go-to guy. He was the one artist we would listen to, read, and sing along with if we could have only one artist. For us, his work was both the mirror and the lamp, the way into so many things that mattered to us.

Although a map of what my synapses were doing that night in the Kettle might have looked very similar to those of *Star Trek*, sports, or other fans when they were with their fellow fans, the stimuli were different. I thought of how Mark Jacobson had written earlier in the decade about Dylan and "this new, bigger world he'd thrust you into."[1] I also thought about what another confessed Dylan fan, University of Virginia English professor Mark Edmundson, had written in *Why Read?*, about what he called "consequential writing." Edmundson was making the case for what makes certain writers more important than others when he stated, "What the defenders of consequential writing need to do is to stand up and say that a Bronte novel can help you live better—can . . . better enhance your expanding circle of self. . . ."[2] I liked the notion, particularly "expanding circle of self," once I substituted "Dylan songs" for "a Bronte novel." I wanted to learn from and with the passionate ones, whatever their ideas of "consequential writing" might be. That particular night in the Village, as had been the case repeatedly in my life, it was Dylan that brought us together.

Thanks to knowing "Changing of the Guards," I was recognized as a member of the tribe who had traveled all the way from central Texas to the Village. It felt good, like I had found yet another home, like I wasn't alone on that desert island and might even someday occupy a position of modest significance there. I didn't want to get too far ahead of myself and start thinking about the possibilities of becoming an island elder. But, after all, let's face it: How many people know that first track off the top of their heads? It was the kind of knowledge that opened the gate to a larger conversational playground.

Going into our second hour in the wood-paneled room where the jukebox played Seventies rock and the Christmas lights twinkled, I was picking up steam when Norma, who appreciates Dylan but, for reasons beyond me, prefers Bach, signaled me that we needed to move on to dinner. All old business had been covered. As far as new business went, we unanimously concurred that the recently released "official bootleg" of "Red River Shore," because of its haunting lyrics about one more complicated love affair and Augie Meyers's transcendent accordion, was a top-five single. We agreed that it was "far too amazing," as Brian put it, to have been originally released twelve years earlier on Dylan's thirtieth studio album, *Time Out of Mind*.

"It would have been the odd man out," Walter said and we nodded in unison.

We talked about the concept of an "official bootleg," as the Dylan industry called part of his catalog, and wondered what other treasures were yet to be unearthed.

We touched upon the rumored piano version of *Street Legal*, "the Holy Grail of bootleggers," according to Nina. We had come full circle to where I had gotten on that evening's roller coaster. I tried to imagine "Changing of the Guards" on piano and hoped that someday I would hear it that way. We made a collective vow to share said rumored version if any of us ever came across it.

Nina, Charlie, Walter, and Brian mentioned that they had tickets for the final three shows of the Tour at the United Palace on November 17, 18, and 19. I briefly wished, as I sometimes do, that we lived in New York and had more money. Walter and I were on the same page regarding Hitchcock's twisted sense of humor and Dylan's send-up of *Psycho* on *Another Side of Bob Dylan* (1964). A sneak preview of what I would say the following night—that Dylan's early and ongoing success was, in large part, due to his underappreciated sense of humor—played well and received a few friendly amendments. The gang stayed on after Norma and I said our good nights and hit the street.

We walked a few blocks out of our way in order to pass 161 West 4th Street, the address of Dylan and Suze Rotolo's apartment back in the *The Freewheelin' Bob Dylan* day. It's a red-brick walk-up with a dingy white door, sitting next to a business called the Four-Faced Liar and across from a tobacco shop run by a Jamaican who, every time I buy my annual pilgrimage cigar from him, tells me that he prefers Bob Marley to Bob Dylan. He probably means it, but I prefer to think he's just messing with me.

There wasn't snow at the corner of Jones and West 4th, like there was when Don Hunstein took the famous photo of Bob and Suze for Columbia Records in February 1963. Nor were we looking much like young Bob with his brown jacket collar turned up and Suze with her green coat and black pants. But, other than those minor details, everything was pretty much perfect. My legs felt like they could go forever. I was with Norma and on my way to MacDougal Street for dinner. We had just had a few beers with my people. For a moment, I felt like we were that floating couple in Chagall's *Above the Town*. "Maybe this is how Bob and Suze felt when they walked these very same streets *long before the stars were torn down*," I told Norma. She saw the air quotes around Bob's words from "Brownsville Girl," squeezed my arm and smiled, happy for me.

I've told that story a lot since that night and begin with it because I continue to wonder who the angel on my shoulder was, how she brought me "Changing of the Guards," and why it matters so much to me. This book is, among other things, an effort to answer those and related questions at the heart of my fifty-year fascination with Dylan's music, words, story, and fans.

Maybe you have a similar long-running connection to Dylan. Many people do. If, however, you are not (yet) a Dylan fan, then perhaps there is another musician or writer or painter or director or actor or athlete who matters deeply, and perhaps a bit mysteriously, to you. Although it is obvious, it nonetheless merits saying that one reason to be a fan—whether it is of Dylan, Dickens, Elvis, or fill-in-the-blank—is to compare notes, explore mysteries, and riff with fellow fans. That was certainly a large part of what was going on in the Kettle that October night. Another Dylan fan, Mark Ellen, came at the question from a slightly different angle earlier that year in *The Word*, a British music magazine, when he wrote: "Is it purely the comfort of a story we already know but just seems to improve with length? Do we take more satisfaction in amassing this arcane information than the knowledge itself affords? . . . And when does it all end?"[3] These are significant rather than rhetorical questions that I will try to answer in the coming pages.

Such questions and a few more, in some shaggy-dog-running-free kind of way, were related to why I was on my way from the Kettle of Fish to Minetta Tavern that October night and to the 92nd Street Y the following one and back into classrooms, libraries, conferences, bookstores, and the Internet for the foreseeable future. I have to come clean: *In Dylan Town* is one more example of another fan unwilling to let the mysteries of fandom be. It is my take on my longest-running fandom.

That take is spread over four chapters. Because this book is primarily a fan study, Dylan and his fans appear in all chapters. Because it is also a memoir, so do I. And, because I am a teacher who teaches courses on not only Dylan but also American culture, I keep returning to questions about teaching and learning and America. When anyone asks me, "Why Dylan?" I say, "He's the writer I care about the most. He's been the way into the best and longest-running conversations I have ever had." I keep returning to Dylan because, like my best teachers and friends through life, he remains central to how I marry what I think and what I feel. I thought of Dylan more than any other person when I read these words from Mark Edmundson in *Why Read?*: "True education . . . ought to fuse the mind and heart."[4]

My opening chapter, "The Varieties of Dylan Fan Experience or: Welcome to Dylan Town," provides an overview of the many ways in which people have been and continue to be Dylan fans. What I have chosen to call informational, personal, and critical approaches have appeared in articles, books, fanzines, websites, and blogs that have come and gone for almost fifty years. To answer one of Mark Ellen's questions, there appears to be no end in sight. While being about Dylan, these responses also raise questions about the appropriate boundaries of fandom by distinguishing between "ideal" and "monster" fans. In the process of writing about these fans, I have looked at my own fandom and its occasional borderline moments as well. In the book's second chapter, "Teaching Dylan," I turn my attention to a few courses that I have taught and a few conference presentations that I have made. Those courses and presentations grew out of a passion that I wanted to share with and model for my students in hopes that they would examine, articulate, and share their own intellectual and spiritual passions both in and, more importantly, beyond school. Chapter Three, "My Back Pages," explores how my growing up led to some of my feelings about Dylan, and how both affected my thoughts about love, marriage, parenthood, work, and living in the material world. Chapter Four, "Dylan Days," is an account of some of the fans and activities surrounding the celebration of Dylan's seventy-second birthday in his North Country hometown. It was there, in May 2013, on Howard Street in Hibbing, Minnesota, that I felt closest to grasping a small part of the mystery that is Dylan, his art, his fans, and my love of it all.

That is a sneak preview of the carpet that you are about to unroll. Before you do so, however, I want to point to a few of its prominent threads. I have not changed names to protect the innocent, and I report all events exactly as I remember them. I confess to enjoying my metaphors quite a bit, and I occasionally even capitalize a few of them. My favorite people—whether in the classroom or in writing, at the table or on the street—are always willing to risk a metaphor. I'm following their lead, but not blaming them for any of my misses. Finally, I am even fonder of quoting the good stuff I find along the way than I am of risking metaphors. Reasonable people might argue that I overdo it. For what it's worth, the same has been said of Dylan by some of his detractors. While knowing that I am not him (in fact, whenever I'm a bit too full of myself, Norma gently and rightly reminds me, "*You're not Him*"), it is part of my calling to share what seems wonderful to me whenever and wherever I am able to do so.

Way back in Grand Prairie, Texas, when I first heard *I'll let you be in my dreams if I can be in yours*, I was hooked. Those words sum up a good bit of what became my learning, teaching, and living philosophies. In that general spirit, I hope that you will view the quotations as gifts, follow them wherever they might lead you, and even feel free to share with me what seems wonderful to you.

This all sounds right to me, at least *most of the time.* Some of the time, however, it also sounds a bit preachy, a little too clever, and slightly, well, defensive. I therefore looked for some reassurance, particularly regarding my quote-happy ways, and found part of what I was hoping for in my friend and teacher Bill Stott's invaluable *Write to the Point* where he raised a question many writers struggle with. Stott asked, "When are quotes worth quoting?" And then answered:

1. When they put words before the reader for close analysis
2. When they are crucial evidence
3. When they say something so well it can't be said better.[5]

I also liked reading David Shields's *Reality Hunger: A Manifesto*, a book that is very much about the courage to quote. Shields turned to Ralph Waldo Emerson on the matter: "A great man quotes bravely and will not draw on his invention when his memory serves him with a word as good. What he quotes, he fills with his own voice and humor."[6] Even though I have no more illusions about being a great man than I do about being Dylan, I do have my aspirations, and I love the kicker about humor.

Throughout *In Dylan Town*, I do my best to acknowledge all my sources. Any time I consciously use Dylan's lyrics I italicize them and have received permission for their use. When I'm quoting Dylan, I'm not trying to be clever or to shoehorn him in wherever I possibly can. It's just how I think and talk. It can be viewed as love or theft, as homage or plagiarism, or something in between all those complicated, charged words. When I quote him, as well as many others who have written words that I admire, I do hope that you hear my respect and affection for them all as well as my own voice and humor.

Finally, I hope *In Dylan Town* has something in common with Joan Didion's "John Wayne: A Love Song," a work of a fan about her fandom. In that essay Didion described meeting Wayne, the man who "rode through my childhood and perhaps through yours" and how she "lost the sense that the face across the table was in certain ways more familiar than my husband's."[7] That resonates with me because Dylan's voices, music, and stories have been in my head—and perhaps in yours—since childhood. He has been to me what John Wayne was to Didion. A title like "Bob Dylan: A Love Song" would probably overstate what I'm up to. But it would do so only by a little.

The following pages are, among other things, my way of thanking not only Dylan but also *all those who've sailed with me*. By the time I finish, perhaps you will even see some of yourself in these pages. Hopefully by then I will have, as novelist Jonathan Lethem had his character Dylan say in *The Fortress of Solitude*, "learned to shut up and play the records."[8] Maybe then you will play your records as well, with slightly new ears and for the people you love. Perhaps, like me, you will be a bit more thankful that Bob Dylan has not only ridden and sailed through our lives but also written and sung for us along the way.

IN DYLAN TOWN

CHAPTER ONE

The Varieties of Dylan Fan Experience or:
Welcome to Dylan Town

On January 1, 2014, Amazon offered 21,238 books, CDs, movies, and other items related to writer-musician-singer-painter-actor-philosopher and self-described "song and dance man" Bob Dylan. Academic Search Complete listed 16,288 articles about him. Collector and archivist Bill Pagel's website www.boblinks.com had been accessed 33,260,467 times since its August 15, 1995, launch. Fifteen blogs and over one hundred "other sites" appeared on http://expectingrain.com, a website named for a Dylan lyric in "Desolation Row" and visited at least once daily by Dylan monofans, as those who focus on only one figure are known in fan studies circles. It is accessed almost as frequently by the rest of us and directs those so inclined to *Bob Links* for "another, even longer, list" of Dylan-based sites. My file cabinets are overflowing and, as these things go, I'm admittedly a very minor collector and an incredibly disorganized archivist.

It is a full-time job, and then some, to keep up with it all. Spreading out everything by and about Dylan would result in something looking like that final shot in *Citizen Kane*, the one of Kane's possessions at Xanadu, a hodgepodge of art and junk, crated and loose, as far as the eye can see—and then much, much, much farther. To put it another way, and in Dylan's words, there's a *lot of water under the bridge, a lot of other stuff too*. But before diving into that water and some of the other stuff too, it makes sense to ask: Who is all of this fuss about?

To start at one beginning, before there were Dylan fans there was Robert Allen Zimmerman. He was born to Beatty and Abe Zimmerman at Saint Mary's Hospital in Duluth, Minnesota, at 9:05 p.m. on May 24, 1941. Legend has it that in October 1959, college freshman Bobby Zimmerman, who had grown up in Hibbing, Minnesota, walked into a Minneapolis coffeehouse called the Ten O'Clock Scholar, approached its owner David Lee about playing there, and, when asked his name by Lee, said, "Bob Dylan." He had developed a repertoire that included the folk songs "Sinner Man," "St. James Infirmary," "Golden Vanity," and the occasional Carter Family tune.[1] Fifteen months later, after withdrawing from the University of Minnesota, he made his way to the coffeehouses and folk clubs of Greenwich Village, as well as to the hospital bedside of his hero of the moment, folk singer Woody Guthrie. By the summer of 1962, Zimmerman had signed with Columbia Records and Witmark Music as well as legally changed his name to Bob Dylan. Over the course of the next four years, right up until a motorcycle accident on July 29, 1966, Dylan released seven albums containing songs that ranged from acoustic anthems of the civil rights and antiwar movements—"Blowin' in the Wind," "Masters of War," and "The Times They Are A-Changin'" among them—to the rock masterpieces "Like a Rolling Stone" and "Desolation Row." He was also performing across the United States and Europe.

Music historian and author of the magisterial *Bob Dylan Encyclopedia*[2] Michael Gray suggested Dylan's cultural impact in these words about *Highway 61 Revisited*: "The whole rock culture, the whole post-Beatle pop-rock world—in an important sense the 1960s started here . . . . It's the carving out of a new emotional correspondence with a new chaos-reality. There it all was in one bombshell of an album, for a generation who only recognized what world they were living in when Dylan illuminated it so piercingly."[3] In September 1965 the cover of *Esquire*, designed by art director George Lois, was titled "The Face of a Hero" and showed a composite image of Dylan, Malcolm X, Fidel Castro, and John F. Kennedy. On that cover and within the pages that followed, Dylan was deemed first among those "who count most with the college rebels." He and his work have been significant parts of cultural conversations ever since.

Dylan famously played electric guitar in 1965, when most of his first fans preferred that he kept playing acoustic. With 1969's *Nashville Skyline*, he turned to country music when the Beatles and most other popular bands were embracing very different sounds and themes. Ten years after his celebrated mid-Sixties trilogy of *Bringing It All Back Home*, *Highway 61 Revisited*, and *Blonde on Blonde* he released *Blood on the Tracks*, arguably his greatest album, and a year later wore whiteface during his performances with a traveling caravan of musicians he led on what he called the Rolling Thunder Revue. A few years after that, having announced his born-again Christianity, he made *Slow Train Coming* (1979) and *Saved* (1980), two albums that again bewildered, and even alienated, many of his fans. At the same time, those albums also brought him some new fans.

On June 7, 1988, in Concord, California, Dylan began his Never Ending Tour with an eye on a younger audience in venues like minor league ballparks and college auditoriums. In 1993, when Bill Clinton was inaugurated, Dylan returned to the Lincoln Memorial, where he had played "When the Ship Comes In" and "Only a Pawn in Their Game" before Martin Luther King Jr.'s "I Have a Dream" speech in 1963. He performed "Chimes of Freedom" as the Clintons applauded and many of us wondered how thirty years had passed so quickly and, even more remarkably, how Dylan was still in the center of it all. Twenty years after that inauguration and upon the Never Ending Tour's twenty-fifth anniversary in 2013, *The Atlantic Cities'* Eric Jaffe described Dylan as "America's most-popular cultural emissary" and calculated that, in his latest incarnation, Dylan had played 2,503 shows in 808 cities and covered 1,007,416 miles.[4] During three of those twenty-five years (from 2006 to 2009) he also recorded sixty episodes of *Theme Time Radio Hour*, his weekly program about American music and culture, as well as publishing the first volume of his memoirs, displaying three series of his paintings, making a few movies, and bringing his number of released albums to sixty.

He has won twelve Grammies, one Academy Award, one Golden Globe, a Pulitzer Prize, a National Medal of Arts, the Presidential Medal of Freedom, and *Chevalier de la Legion d'honneur*. The odds on his winning the Nobel Prize for Literature improve each year. In 2013 London bookmakers made him a 50-1 bet, as were Margaret Atwood, Salman Rushdie, Don DeLillo, Philip Roth, William Trevor, and Cormac McCarthy.

As the bookies have gone, so have the bookish. Kevin J. H. Dettmar introduced *The Cambridge Companion to Bob Dylan*[5] with the following claim: "[N]o popular-culture figure has ever been adopted into the curricula of colleges and university language and literature departments in the way Dylan has; critics have called James Joyce 'God's gift to English departments,' but Dylan is no less deserving of that designation."[6]

As I write this, Dylan has just announced that he will begin his 2014 schedule with two weeks of shows in Tokyo, Sapporo, Nagoya, Fukuoka, and Osaka. No one has kept working and playing at such a level for so many years. Nor has anyone else delighted and frustrated and challenged us so many times. In our time, no one has been quoted and argued over more.

Given the richness of Dylan's art and life, it is no wonder that Dylan Town—as I call the space defined by what Dylan fans say, do, and make—has grown at such a phenomenal rate. It is overflowing with noise and activity and of interest not only to fans who spend much of their time there but also to students and teachers of popular culture who visit for a while. Like every other space where people come together, Dylan Town has its zones with their notable characters and distinct timbres. When seen and heard whole, it suggests what it means to be a Dylan fan and demonstrates how some popular artists are as consequential as traditionally canonical writers. Finally, it contains clues about why and how Dylan matters to people over time, across generations, and around the world.

When I talk about Dylan Town I describe its population differently than does Ian Crouch, who posted *Dylan TV*, a *New Yorker* blog about Vania Heymann's witty 2013 interactive music video that, according to the *Telegraph*, had over seventy million views.[7] The video featured footage of performers voicing the lyrics to "Like a Rolling Stone" on sixteen channels of simulated cable television programs that parodied the Shopping Network, ESPN, the History Channel, and several other options. Midway through *Dylan TV*, Crouch described people interested in Dylan: "For years, the question of who Bob Dylan is has been asked again and again by critics and fans and obsessives."[8] This is one way of categorizing people interested in Dylan.

Mark Jacobson's 2001 *Rolling Stone* article "Tangled Up in Bob" proposed another three-part division. According to Jacobson, "[w]ritten Dylanology breaks down into three camps"—those who "ignore the Living Bob altogether" and emphasize cultural context, those who "take the middle path, acknowledging the Living Bob's presence, while warily wishing not to unduly trespass on the artist's personal space," and those who "go forward, to stand naked before him demanding his attention."[9]

My trinity of Dylan people comes from yet another point of view. It is neither based upon the kind of relationships we have with normalcy nor the kind of relationship we seek with Dylan. Instead, I see *all* of us as fans, which is but one of Crouch's groups, and am interested in what we have written, said, and done about Dylan over the years. I believe that those labors of love, even the more questionable and troubling ones, can be viewed as predominately informational, personal, or critical. Admittedly, my categories, like Crouch's and Jacobson's, bleed into one another. After all, one person's critic is another's obsessive, the line between the personal and the critical is very much in the eye of the beholder, and, thankfully, we have Venn diagrams to handle that which may be both fish and fowl.

My point is that it all comes from "fans," at least as the word is defined by Mark Duffett, author of *Understanding Fandom: An Introduction to the Study of Media Fan Culture*.[10] Duffett describes a fan as "a self-identified enthusiast, devotee or follower of a particular media genre, text, person or activity."[11] This genus can accommodate plenty of species, however tricky naming those species may be. Fortunately, there are some guides along our way.

One of them, Henry Jenkins III, opened *Textual Poachers*, his 1992 groundbreaking study of fans, with the following words that apply to Dylan fans as much as they do to any other self-identified enthusiasts, devotees, or followers: "[F]an culture is a complex, multidimensional phenomenon, inviting many forms of participation and levels of engagement."[12] He described fans—of whatever genres, texts, or individuals—as active and mindful. At the time, this was a large step in countering the popular notion that all fans were mad men and women in attics or pathetic characters in their parents' basements. "Fan reading," Jenkins argued, "is a social process through which individual interpretations are shaped and reinforced through ongoing discussions with other readers."[13] He delighted in noting, "[T]hey are also 'nomads' [who are] constantly advancing upon another text, appropriating new materials, making new meanings."[14] Lively discussions between fans, the "social process" that is such an essential aspect of Jenkins's observation, and the various meanings that grow out of those discussions play out in a variety of contexts. They take place at professional meetings and informal meet-ups; on websites and blogs; in books, fanzines, and peer-reviewed journals. They have increased at an astounding rate over the course of Dylan's career and are where to find and listen to his fans.

On Google, the first stop for so many explorations in 2014, the first entry for Bob Dylan is www.bobdylan.com, which describes itself as the "[o]fficial Bob Dylan website featuring Bob Dylan news, music, books, album info, tour dates and more." The "official" information that appears there consists of press releases from Dylan and his staff, concert dates, authorized lyrics, and available merchandise. Those looking for "more" than these bare bones quickly find their way to www.boblinks.com and http://expectingrain.com. Like www.bobdylan.com, these websites provide information about concert dates, set lists, and Dylan history. Their real appeal, however, is that they branch out into the vast ecosystem surrounding Dylan's art and life. Like *Isis*, which is currently the longest-running Dylan fanzine, the sites are devoted to making as much Dylan-related material—other sites, blogs, discussion forums, images, tape-trading opportunities—available with as little editorial comment as possible.

The individuals behind these ways of seeing and sharing Dylan—the Informers as I think of them—are Bill Pagel in Minnesota at *Bob Links*, Karl Erik

Andersen in Sweden at *Expecting Rain*, and the publisher-editor of *Isis*, Derek Barker, in the United Kingdom. They are the relatively anonymous heroes of Dylan Town. They steer fans to the information that leads to new delights or dead ends and many things in between. Michael Gray praises each of them in *The Bob Dylan Encyclopedia*. He describes Pagel as "[a] *serious* collector and archivist" and calls *Bob Links* "an invaluable website . . . which provides uncannily up-to-date information on Dylan's concert performances."[15] Andersen "runs one of the most extraordinary, copious Dylan websites of all the hundreds that are out there in cyberspace," posting twice daily "every web page that mentions Bob Dylan's name and a number of extra ones that he thinks will interest people keen enough to be regular visitors to the site 'and even maybe the man himself.'"[16] For the past four years virtual visitors to his http//expectingrain.com have exceeded eight million annually (which, for what it's worth, is twice the number of people who have physically visited the Grand Canyon over the same period). First-time visits to the website have grown at the impressive rate of 100,000 annually over the past decade. On their websites, Pagel and Andersen have been content to keep their thoughts about "the man himself," as Andersen described Dylan, to themselves. They have left personal responses and critical analyses to others who have such dispositions and find the places to express them.

In recent years, *Isis* has been one such place. It did not, however, begin that way. Started a full decade before Google, *Bob Links*, and *Expecting Rain*, it was named by Barker for Dylan's song about turquoise, gold, and a marriage. The magazine's initial purpose was "to find and give out information rather than to offer critical assessment."[17] Barker viewed *Isis* as a way "to communicate with my ever-growing circle of friends." Dylan fans would send him snippets of news that he would collect and then redistribute in a newsletter. According to Barker, "This *free* exchange of information continued for more than two years, until the sheer volume of participants and news made it impossible to continue in this vein."[18] The bulletin then turned into a magazine that could be purchased by subscription and, eventually, in bookstores. The guiding principle of "exchange of information" remained, even as the word *free* was slightly redefined.

Isis is currently filled with photographs, brief interviews, and historical information related to Dylan. There are editors and contributors, but their voices are rarely, if ever, conspicuous. For instance, "The Robert Shelton Minnesota Transcripts," primary material from one of Dylan's earliest biographers, appeared in 1999, thirteen years after the publication of Shelton's book. It began with the following understated introduction: "As far as we at *Isis* are aware, this is the only interview ever given by Abram Zimmerman and the only full interview given by Beatty Zimmerman."[19] What readers then got was Shelton's transcription of Dylan's parents describing the early days of their famous first son's life. This was but one example of providing fans, the very word Barker used to describe himself in his editor's introduction to a collection of *Isis* articles, access to information that, up until then, they had only seen paraphrased. For many of us, reading "The first part is twenty-six pages of double-spaced typing on foolscap paper; it is labelled 'TAPE IV' and headed '*Side One*'" was like watching a curtain from another time and place open to reveal a treasure, one that enriched our sense of where Dylan's earliest music came from.[20] *Foolscap* was almost as good as abracadabra. Excitement in the presence of such admittedly small, but also delightful, moments is part of what differentiates true fans from casual listeners. They add layers and texture to fan knowledge and appreciation, as well as furnish more grist for the collective mill, which runs on layers and textures.

In another issue of *Isis*, fans could get a picture of "Dylan's Village" from Barker and Bob Levinson's collaboration. Written in the matter-of-fact, third-person house style, it mapped the significant chronology and landmarks of Dylan's initial Greenwich Village days and brought to mind black-and-white photographs of a long-gone downtown. It was the kind of place we want to know about not only because Dylan was there but also because it was interesting in its own right—romantic and mysterious with all kinds of people passing through, some of them possibly even our blood relatives from long ago and far away.

But *Isis* could not sustain itself on recreating historical moments. In a marketplace where fans can get their information the very next day at not only http://expectingrain.com but also at Harold Lepidus's blog *Bob Dylan Examiner*, the fanzine had to alter its original course slightly. Along with the information and photographs that now occupy the majority of its pages, personal accounts of fans are published periodically under the recurring title "Close Encounters." Tales of Dylan sightings have also found homes in other fanzines and even been the organizing principle for Tracy Johnson's *Encounters with Bob Dylan: If You See Him, Say Hello*,[21] which Barker introduced by writing, "For the first time, the people that really matter, the fans, are given a chance to tell their stories."[22]

The point is that everyone in Dylan Town—those who provide the information, those who take a more overtly personal approach to Dylan's life and art, and those who engage in various forms of criticism of it all—has a story to tell.

All of these stories grow out of individual enthusiasms, the varieties of which have always interested, moved, and called me. Many of the best moments of my life have revolved around being in the presence of enthusiasts sharing and performing their passions—my father taking me on rounds at the hospital or to bookstores or showing me around New York City; Rodney J. Kidd telling stories at Friday Mountain Boys Camp; Willie Mays playing center field for the Giants or Arnold Palmer sinking a birdie putt; Mr. Wallis teaching eighth-grade world history; Mrs. Powell translating high school Latin; Walter Sokel lecturing about Kafka; T. B. L. Webster describing fifth-century Athens; Wick Wadlington discussing Melville in his graduate seminar; countless musicians (most memorably, Dylan, Bruce Springsteen, Leonard Cohen, Van Morrison, Joni Mitchell, David Byrne, and Elvis Costello) performing live; the words of Herman Melville, Gabriel García Márquez, and Michael Chabon coming off the page; Norma organizing family gatherings or seeing her favorite paintings; our kids enthusing over Corvettes or fashion or robotics or food. I always got caught up in what I was seeing, hearing, reading, or doing and wanted to feel that kind of transport as much as possible (which, by the way, perhaps explains why "Mr. Tambourine Man," with its *In the jingle jangle morning I'll come followin' you*, is my favorite Dylan song).

I still do. It wasn't a very big step from wanting that feeling to wanting to find ways to share that kind of experience with others whenever and however I could. In short, I am a congenital and incurable enthusiast, a natural-born fan, and one more storyteller in Dylan Town.

The word "enthusiast" appears in both Duffett's definition of a fan and in the "Social Phenomena" section of the *Continuum Encyclopedia of Popular Music in the World* in which Chris Atton defines fanzines as "an amateur form of publishing, one that is prompted less by commercial gain than by enthusiasm for its subject."[23] As both fate and something special about Dylan's art would have it, Atton then invoked Dylan fans as his specific example. "Fans of rock auteurs such as Bob Dylan," he states, "have continued to find the *oeuvres* of their favorite artists inexhaustible as sites for criticism, documentation and speculation. . . . They offer a space for the creation, development and enacting of a community of interest."[24]

Robert Strachan, editor of *Popular Music History*, also linked Dylan, his fans, and their fanzines to a point that opens up how we learn from and teach one another in our communities of interest. In "'Where Do I Begin the Story?': Collective Memory, Biographical Authority, and the Rock Biography," Strachan put *No Direction Home*, Robert Shelton's 1986 biography of Dylan, in conversation with "the proliferation of Dylan fanzines, newsletters and societies" and concluded that "biographical authority becomes unstable" in such a lively critical environment. "The roles of expert and analyst are thrown into crisis in an area where analytic and possessive discourses are widely used among fans."[25]

In other words, in a truly wide-open democracy of information, one where expertise is up for grabs, we can all be fans. How we respond to and what we make of the information determines what kinds of fans we are and what kinds of conversations we value. Peter Coviello put it this way in a 2012 article about the band Steely Dan: "Part of what's so exhilarating . . . is that in this scene of talk, there are no experts, only enthusiasts and coconspirators . . . at the table of joy."[26]

"The table of joy" would fit right in the kind of world Dylan evoked at the conclusion of his radio episode about friends and neighbors. He was talking about music but, as so often seems the case, so much more when he said, "We don't need any border patrols or people trying to pigeonhole music. We just need more records like [War's 'Why Can't We Be Friends?']." Since hearing that, I've been saying "we don't need any border patrols" every chance I get. It is one more way of talking about making room in our conversations and classrooms for more people and their different enthusiasms, for recognizing that "it's all one song," as Willie Nelson told journalist Adam Gopnik.[27]

Coviello's, Dylan's, and Nelson's words also made me think that listening to Dylan is never just about Dylan. As Paul Williams, creator of *Crawdaddy*, the first American rock magazine, put it, "In many ways, understanding Dylan has a lot to do with understanding yourself."[28] Williams was eighteen years old when he wrote those words in his review of *Blonde on Blonde*. He stated that "[u]nderstanding is feeling"[29] and described himself as, first and foremost, "a fan"[30] writing "personal reports. Usually written to others who I imagined felt similar excitement. Sometimes not just reports from the front, but conversations on the front. Did you hear what I heard?"[31] Williams asked and then answered such questions for the next thirty years in a variety of publications and four books about Dylan. He was early, but hardly alone, in accentuating the personal and connecting it to the social. In the words of Michael Gray, many "Dylan aficionados" found Williams's style "hopelessly gushing and somewhat *Californian*" before concluding that others appreciated his "breadth of knowledge matched by percipience as well as passion."[32]

Personal reports with a communal awareness, albeit less "gushing," were also a significant part of the *Telegraph*, a British Dylan fanzine that ran from 1981 to 1997 and described by Gray as "the finest Dylan fanzine there's ever been."[33] Jonathan Cott concurred in his introduction to Rolling Stone Press's *Bob Dylan*.[34] He stated that the *Telegraph* was "the first and last word on every matter—from the sublime to the inane and from fact to hearsay—that has anything to do with Dylan."[35]

The *Telegraph* was founded and edited by John Bauldie, a college lecturer in English literature, who was also "keen on Phil Ochs, David Blue, Neil Young, Bruce Springsteen, Roger McGuinn and a number of other singer-songwriters, and . . . himself an amateur guitarist and songwriter."[36] The *Telegraph*'s origins, as Bauldie described them on a web page, grew out of his admiration for "a newsletter called *The Wicked Messenger* [for being] an excellent thing—funny, informative, endlessly fascinating." That blend of all things Dylan and contributors' voices—"funny, informative, endlessly fascinating"—became the house style, just as providing information and downplaying voice characterized *Isis* and Williams's California-inflected passion marked his writing.

Things started went well enough at the *Telegraph*. Then Bauldie met A. J. Weberman, who called himself the world's only living Dylanologist. Bauldie described him as "the Bob Dylan fan who'd become a monster."[37] Their New York meeting in the summer of 1982 caused Bauldie and his colleagues to reflect upon the nature of their undertaking at the *Telegraph*. At the heart of the matter were questions about boundaries and the roles that fans take on in policing one another. It was a question about Dylan fans with implications about anyone and everyone else's fans.

Brooklyn-born Weberman had dropped out of college in the mid-Sixties to devote his life to interpreting Dylan. For the next two decades, he claimed to be working on a tome he called the *Dylan Concordance*, a volume that he promised would decode every Dylan message and solve every related mystery. Over the course of his undertaking, he had also organized the Dylan Liberation Front and held a street party outside Dylan's apartment on Dylan's thirtieth birthday in 1971. He also managed to rummage through Dylan's garbage searching for evidence to support his theory that Dylan was a heroin addict. His other claim to dubious fame was that Dylan supposedly attacked him on MacDougal Street.[38] He was a notorious character in Dylan Town and living proof that not all fans are good fans.

Bauldie wrote "A Meeting with A. J. Weberman, Summer of '82" about a few hours they spent together walking in Greenwich Village and going to Weberman's apartment. It read like an Edgar Allan Poe horror tale crossed with a Rod Serling *Twilight Zone* episode. As reported by Bauldie, Weberman's paranoia crept deep. Closed-circuit cameras, tear-gas canisters, large dogs, and mysterious archives wove through the descriptions of Weberman's Greenwich Village apartment. Although Gray described the story as "affectionate,"[39] it struck me as melancholy and creepy. However one reads it, according to Bauldie Weberman and his behavior caused the *Telegraph*'s writers to look in the mirror and to do "a lot of soul-searching and breast-beating—sometimes both at once." Their conversations about where admiration crossed over into obsession "raged in the pages of *The Telegraph*" where they asked themselves, "Were we all involved in a pursuit that was ultimately unworthy? Was there ignominy in being a fan?"[40]

Such questions come with the territory, as Derek Barker noted in "A Close Encounter of the Shocking Kind." Rather than the usual breezy, feel-good account of a random sighting of Dylan that appeared in *Isis*, Barker wrote about Mark David Chapman, John Lennon's assassin, and the possibility that he may have targeted Dylan in 1979. He went on to propose that Dylan's 1981 *Shot of Love* was inspired by the Lennon assassination. In support of that argument, Barker pointed to the pop-art rendering of an explosion on the album cover and then quoted Dylan telling journalists at a press conference in Travemünde, in July 1981, "He [Lennon] was actually shot by someone who supposedly loved him. But what kind of love is that? That's fan love. That's what hero worship can breed, if you worship a man in that kind of way."[41]

Like Dylan, Barker and Bauldie were increasingly concerned that the ways some fans expressed their personal attachments went beyond quirky to unhealthy. Playwright and actor Sam Shepard, who joined the 1975 Rolling Thunder Revue at Dylan's request, wrote from the inside of that tour about Dylan's fans and particularly about the potential monsters out there in Dylan's audiences. These few, haunting words in his *Rolling Thunder Logbook*[42] accompany a photograph of Dylan signing autographs for some of his fans: "Fans are more dangerous than a man with a weapon because they're after something invisible. Some imagined 'something.' At least with a gun you know what you're facing."[43] Shepard neither searched his soul nor beat his breast about his observation. "[S]omething invisible. Some imagined 'something'" carries a lot of weight. It also cuts a number of ways.

Weberman went through Dylan's trash looking for it. Other fans trespassed when Dylan was living in Woodstock trying to find it. Throughout his career,

Dylan has worried not only for his and his family's privacy but also for his and their safety. One Dylan admirer, Richard Williams, wrote of how admirers could cross over: "At one extreme, there are said to be more than 500 Bob Dylan fans logged in a police computer file because they've indicated that they'd like to do him some sort of physical harm."[44]

Dylan was not the only object of fans gone wrong. Charles Manson heard what he heard in "Helter Skelter." John Lennon was killed outside his apartment. George Harrison was attacked and stabbed in his home by Michael Abram. Unfortunately, there is also the case of J. D. Salinger and a few of his most notorious fans. In *Salinger*,[45] David Shields and Shane Salerno link Mark David Chapman, John Hinckley (who wounded President Ronald Reagan), and Robert Bardo (who killed actress Rebecca Schaeffer) to their adorations of *The Catcher in the Rye*. These are examples of searchers gone so wrong, "monster" fans, that they raise questions for all of us who are fans and also looking for something that is invisible.

At the *Telegraph*, in response to such questions, they decided that what their kinds of fans should be doing was not abandon ship but rather provide "everything that the discerning Dylan fan might need. And some stuff that the dDf [as Bauldie abbreviated the ideal] couldn't possibly live without."[46] One such dDf was Roy Kelly. His writing showed what discernment, as distinguished from stalking, looked like. "Fans, Collectors and *Biograph*" was published upon the occasion of Dylan's 1985 release and described it as "both a monument to, and a mockery of, information-amassing. This neat box-set of records shows us that life is a mess of mistakes and more."[47] He spoke to the dilemma inherent in a fan having everything, from first editions to unofficial bootlegs to literal garbage. For him, *Biograph* raised "the issue of what it *means* to be an admirer, a fan, a critic, a collector."[48] His answer, with its three prescriptive *should*s, is an articulation of healthy fandom and merits lengthy quotation:

> So we fans and collectors should seize upon *Biograph* as an opportunity not to be proprietorial, not to think because we may know every interviewed word he's said over the last twenty-plus years (how dreadful if someone confronted you with the same documentation) that Bob Dylan should somehow be under our control. All we should do, all we can do, is try to listen with an intelligent heart to what is produced, and to know what makes it good or bad.[49]

Kelly finished his review by returning to why he valued *what is produced*. He listened to and read the words and then described Dylan as "a mystery and a funny wonder, and there's no one else like him ... a mystic [who] writes about what it's like to be human, seeking God and coming to terms with human flawed love."[50]

"[A] mystery and a funny wonder" made me wish that I had been in those rooms listening to him, Bauldie, Gray, and their Dylan friends. I also wanted to find more of what Kelly had written. His words put me on another trail, sent me in a new direction, which is what our best teachers, favorite artists, and soul mates do. Like Paul Williams, Kelly demonstrated that listening with "an intelligent heart"[51] was crucial to the difference between the ideal fan and the monster fan and one way to distinguish between invisible somethings like Williams' "understanding" and Shepard's "danger." Kelly's description of Dylan gave me language for what I sensed Dylan brought out in many of his best fans.

Those fans, listening with intelligent hearts, might even produce "wholly new works of creativity," as college professor William Carpenter put it when he wrote about requiring his students to "re-purpose a Dylan song."[52] The assignment, which Carpenter described in "Bob Dylan and the New Humanities" for the fanzine *Montague Street*, required students to do what Dylan, from the very beginning of his career and repeatedly thereafter, had urged his listeners to do: make their own meanings rather than look to him for explanations of his words or of their worlds. Carpenter then took it a step further by requiring them to share those meanings with others and thereby to be part of a conversation. I could see a straight line from his assignment to Coviello's table of joy.

I also wondered how I would deal with being seated next to, say, A. J. Weberman rather than Roy Kelly at that metaphorical table. Given that I was proposing that there be no border patrol in Dylan Town, I also felt that I had to be willing to sit next to whoever was there and to play the cards I was dealt. In short, I had to find a way to listen with an intelligent heart to those with whom I disagreed as well as with my kindred spirits. And, once again, more of Kelly's words—"to know what makes it good or bad"—came to my rescue. The "it," the "what was produced," in this case was the work of my fellow Dylan fans.

The first places I looked for what fans had produced were Tracy Johnson's *Encounters with Bob Dylan: If You See Him, Say Hello*,[53] a collection of fan stories, and *My Bob Dylan Story ...!*, a website established by doctoral researcher Barry Williams in 2012. Johnson's book is weighted heavily toward individuals who discovered Dylan early in his career and their lives. Most of her storytellers tended to be older than fifty and to have been longtime fans. Women described him as "speaking my language"[54] and "getting us . . . into our own minds."[55] Men used words like "charismatic"[56] and "mesmerizing."[57] Four of the accounts contained the phrase "changed forever."[58] As would be the case in any gathering, a few voices stood out.

One belonged to Pamela Des Barres, author of *I'm with the Band: Confessions of a Groupie.*[59] As she told it, she and her friend Joycie ran into Dylan in 1987 "at a little party at a cool soul-food joint on Pico" and ended up at his Malibu birthday party, where "[d]ogs woof, children laugh, the sun glints and sparkles on the sea."[60] Tom Petty, Debra Winger, "various cool musicians, hip record-business types . . . [and] GEORGE HARRISON!" showed up. Joycie took Des Barres's picture with Dylan. Johnson printed the picture to accompany Des Barres's account, and Dylan looked distracted, at best, in the black-and-white snapshot. By the end of her tale filled with dropped names and made-for-television descriptions, Des Barres revealed that although she had "paired up" with Jim Morrison, Mick Jagger, Keith Moon, Jimmy Page, Gram Parsons, Waylon Jennings, and a few other musicians over the years, she never did so with Dylan, whom she described as both her "hero" and "goofy." It was all, in her words, "a bit overwhelming, all very charming and tra-la."[61] Uncertain of what to make of the *tra-la*, I was left thinking that Des Barres, whom I can only respond to on the basis of her words on the page, had produced an example of a kind of false intimacy that a fan might desire with her or his "hero," goofy or otherwise.

Another cautionary tale of an aspiring Dylan groupie, by Larry Sloman in *On the Road with Bob Dylan,*[62] demonstrated that a related type of intimacy was far from tra-la. Sloman wrote 461 pages about the Rolling Thunder Revue and ended his book with his sixteenth entry about "Lisa (Dylan fan)," as she is listed in the index. Lisa is first described as "young, real sad-eyed, with a large feathered hat topping off her post-hippie garb."[63] The more she appears throughout the book, it is clear she is important to Sloman's story. At one point he wrote his editor at *Rolling Stone*, in which his book originated, about her significance. He stated that he was striving to capture "the spirit of the tour" and added, "[I]t covers it, that stuff about Lisa. She's a prototype on this tour. I'm a sociologist."[64] The sociologist from *Rolling Stone* let us see the prototype nine more times before giving her the book's final words, by way of her letter to him. According to Sloman, along the way Lisa had helped round up groupies for a scene in Dylan's movie *Renaldo and Clara*, appeared in a hospitality suite in Quebec, shifted her designs upon Dylan to musician Roger McGuinn, and been cruelly nicknamed the Queen of the Shutouts. Her letter, which may have been as much a literary device from a prototype as a historical document from a source, ended:

> Well, I'm really fucked up and I'm just writing the first things that come into my head so if I keep on it'll be a 10 page letter about nothing. Write to me and tell me what's happening. Oh, I asked T-Bone [Burnett, another musician with the Revue] about the song they wrote about me and he said if I didn't hear it in the future, I'd hear it in the pasture. That's a good line. Take care. Love, Lisa.[65]

It was a good line but also part of a disheartening tale of a fan whose behavior had become the butt of others' jokes.

One more Dylan fan who walked the line between being laughed with and laughed at was Mel Prussack, a retired pharmacist from Old Bridge, New Jersey. His story appeared in *Encounters with Bob Dylan* in which he described making a "Mr. Tambourine Man" Zim-Art hat, "Dyl-Time" clocks, and twice winning first place in the Dylan Imitators Contest in Greenwich Village. He kept a shrine to Dylan at his home and was one of the most productive makers of fan art in Dylan Town. As I read about what Prussack was doing I thought of Henry Jenkins describing the fan labor that is known as "filk" and the way it "suggests . . . the translation of program material into new texts that more perfectly serve fan interests, the sense of possession the fan feels toward favored media products, the celebration of intense emotional commitments."[66] That sounded pretty good to me. I was finding Prussack pretty harmless.

However, as I continued reading Prussack's account my assessment shifted. Prussack stated, "Dylan knows who I am . . . I've been told that he refers to me as 'the nut from New Jersey,' which I feel is a big compliment. I've never had the chance to meet him, but I've certainly tried. I've gone to his bus and tried to get in there, and I've hung out around his house, but it's very difficult."[67] That final sentence suddenly made the last part of Jenkins's quote about filk—"and the religious fervor that links fandom to its roots in fanaticism"[68]—appropriate and slightly haunting.

Fortunately, the majority of fans in *Encounters with Bob Dylan* and *On the Road with Bob Dylan* were far less needy and far more aware of the boundaries between themselves and Dylan. Among those who were neither self-proclaimed groupies nor "nuts from New Jersey" was Andy Miller, a practicing educational psychologist who admired Dylan's language so much that he avoided seeing him perform for fear that it would break a spell he had been under for years. In Johnson's chapter titled "Series of Dreams," Miller recounted being seventeen years old and claimed that he remembered watching Dylan perform "Blowin' in the Wind" on "Sunday Night at the London Palladium." That night "my world changed. I was pulled across mountains and oceans by the emotion in the words and melody . . . . That may have been the beginning of my reluctance to acknowledge the source of this much power as merely flesh and blood."[69] When Miller finally went with his two teenage sons to see Dylan perform at Wembley, he realized, "Once, I didn't want to be just another person burdening him with the responsibility of my appreciation, adding to that overwhelming stock of expectations heaped upon him" and continued, "I had also started out with that strange fear that the enormity of his work would somehow be diminished for me if I had living, breathing evidence that it really did originate in one man."[70] By the end of the evening Miller concluded that "the magnitude of his achievement is undiminished."[71] That was Johnson's final chapter in *Encounters with Bob Dylan* and a healthy counterweight to the more eccentric tales.

Refreshingly, and in keeping with my suspicion that Dylan's fans span generations, young people were as numerous on Barry Williams's 2012 website *My Bob Dylan Story . . .!* as they were scarce in Johnson's book. They even merited their own link as Bob's Younger Fans. Williams's "ethnographic approach and phenomenological methodology" expanded upon what Derek Barker started at *Isis* and what Tracy Johnson continued in *Encounters with Bob Dylan*. Williams, a working and teaching sociologist at Aston University, gathered fan stories and incorporated them into his research. At *My Bob Dylan Story . . .!* respondents were mostly, and in equal parts, from the United States and Europe. Men outnumbered women approximately four to one, and the role of the Internet in building "the Dylan community" was frequently mentioned. So was "feeling like I was born decades too late." Dylan was repeatedly described as a "teacher," "sorcerer," and "musical god."[72]

Angus, seventeen and from Scotland, described himself as a child of YouTube and being "entranced by a video of 'Mr. Tambourine Man' at Newport." Another teenager recalled seeing a CD-ROM of Dylan singing "It's All Over Now, Baby Blue" when she was five, getting the album *Time Out of Mind* for her seventh birthday, becoming tired of Dylan by the time she was eleven, and returning to him as a late teen when she "remember[ed] the songs I had heard as a kid."

Many wrote of sharing Dylan with their parents and of being introduced to roots music and Beat poetry through his work.[73]

Williams also conducted a "short survey," asking respondents the following open-ended questions: "What does Bob Dylan mean to you?" "Are Dylan fans any different from other music fans?" "In what ways?"[74] When I, discerning Dylan fan that I fancy myself, saw these questions, I had visions of a gold mine of personal responses out there in Williams's data. As Dylan put it in "Isis," *I was thinkin' about turquoise, I was thinkin' about gold / I was thinkin' about diamonds and the world's biggest necklace.* As it turned out, I was right, in a limited sort of way.

Five thousand people from sixty-four countries responded in fifty-four languages, demonstrating that Dylan Town is, among other things, quite the melting pot. What the answers added up to, according to the pie charts on the website, is that 33.7 percent of my global neighbors stated that Dylan's music influenced their personal lives to "a great extent." I would have been with them rather than the 32.6 percent who answered "quite a lot," 26.4 percent who selected "somewhat-sometimes," and 7.3 percent who opted for "not really at all."[75]

One of my first blushes was that it would be very interesting to see how other fans of other figures would answer the question. My hunch, based on my reading of the measured narrative responses that Dylan fans gave Williams, is that the percentage of to "a great extent" of fans-of-others would probably be larger. Several of Williams's respondents expressed uneasiness, even shame, about being labeled "fans." Deadheads and the fans of Elvis and Springsteen do not express such feelings in such high number.[76] Many of the voices that emerged from the short survey, like the writers at the *Telegraph*, were uneasy with the word *fan*. In fact, this emerged as perhaps one of the primary ways in which Dylan fans are different from other fans.

I, too, have had that feeling more times and for longer than I like to admit. After all, I'm a card-carrying academic who wrote my master's thesis on Melville rather than, as I was tempted to do, on Joni Mitchell. And my dissertation was on American writers in Paris after World War II rather than, as my mentor Bill Stott urged me to make it, on music in Austin in the 1970s. Those doctoral defense questions ("Why should we care about popular culture, Mr. Gaines? Really, why?") had returned to me repeatedly over the years.

As I read the answers of Williams's respondents I realized that, in spite of my delight in studying and sharing Dylan's art, I too had too long viewed it as a guilty pleasure. I had bought into a particular canon, an established definition of cultural capital that came with its own border patrol. And why shouldn't I? I loved *Moby-Dick*, Faulkner, and much of what I was supposed to love. That was where the reward system lay in the groves of academe. But I also loved Dylan and movies and sports in many of the same ways and, truth be told, sometimes even more deeply. What I most wanted to do was to embrace it all.

I wrote Mark Duffett, author of *Understanding Fandom*, about fan unease and particularly as it related to Dylan fans. He cautiously confirmed my hypothesis: "While it is dangerous to generalize about these things, Dylan does tend to attract a more middle class fan base, some of whom might be uncomfortable with the idea of fandom itself."[77] He then helped me frame my topic: "I suppose the question to ask here is: how (and for who) does fandom specifically for Dylan allow access to pleasures that certain kinds of sensibility might otherwise deny."[78]

Such a sensibility could be seen in the answers to the question about how Dylan fans were different from other music fans, answers in which I recognized many of my own responses over the years. The descriptors "intellectuals," "thinkers," and having "a literary bent" recurred. One respondent put it this way: "He's full of puzzles, and full of truths. He's forever changing and challenging his audiences." That, too, sounded familiar to me. Many took Dylan as the embodiment of a particular kind of individualism, one for "playful word freaks." One young fan described him as "just so sweet and smart and funny" while another stated, "I don't know what other music fans are like really. Dylanfreaks to me seem to be the only ones who have a sense of humour. Tell a Beatles fan that they were rubbish live and they'll cut your head off. Tell a Dylan fan and they'll reminisce about the worst Dylan shows they've been at." These personal responses and particularly their emphases upon ironic self-awareness were in keeping with what Duffett wrote me about "issues like class and cultural capital" and what made Dylan in particular appealing to readers and writers of many sorts, me among them.

On the other hand, there were clearly fan stories I could not have written for several reasons. Harold F. Weiner, who took one of Bob Levinson's New School Dylan classes, wrote one such book titled *Tangled Up in Tunes: Ballad of a Dylanhead*.[79] It is a personal account of being both a Deadhead and a Dylan fan. Calling himself "Catfish," a nickname his fellow Deadheads gave him for his air guitar jam to the band's "Catfish John," much of Weiner's memoir is about finding Dylan by way of his fondness for the Grateful Dead. Along the way and amid all the descriptions of drugs, cleavages, car crashes, sexual conquests, and buffet dinners, he provided a few broad strokes about the differences between the two groups of fans that his title tantalizingly suggested. He affectionately described his fellow Deadheads as "wiry misfits with beards and pony-tails [and] braless ladies twirling and flailing their arms like ballerinas."[80] His following the Dead was in many ways a communal one, both in terms of being with his buddies at numerous shows and of knowing many of the regulars and their rituals at those shows. By his own account, they all took the same drugs and wore very similar clothes.

Tellingly, this was not the case during his Dylan days. At the book's one point of explicit comparison between Dylan and the Dead he observed, "Our [Deadhead] road trips were musical pilgrimages that resulted in bootleg orgies—lots of male bonding. I liked my new role as the stranger in town following Dylan."[81] That momentary insight, while only one person's story, jibed with what a lot of Dylan fans had told both Johnson and Williams about being, in the words of Dylan, *on your own.*

Another writer and fan, novelist Michael Chabon, came at Dylan from a different direction when he described having received Dylan's album *Desire* for his thirteenth birthday. He remembered "the mysterious record jacket. . . . On the front there was a fey Jewish cowboy in furs and windblown scarves; on the back, Tarot cards and a hermetic set of liner notes shorn of punctuation, in all but illegible type."[82] Chabon then took his readers to something larger than himself or Dylan: "At thirteen, you put on a record for the first time with not merely a dire hope but a good possibility that it is somehow going to alter the course of your life." When the needle landed on that particular piece of vinyl, he "recognized, in the ache and the ardor of that windblown, Jewish-cowboy voice, the contours of a world I was just beginning to know."[83] Ten years later, upon the occasion of Dylan's being the first musician inducted into the American Academy of Arts and Letters, Chabon returned to "the ache and rasp of that all-too-human-voice, now snarling, now weary, now sweet, now brokenhearted." He finished his tribute by describing his own desire, as a writer at the beginning of a remarkable career of his own, for "a voice as full of fire and longing and wit as Bob Dylan's."[84]

It is difficult to imagine a more concise and spot-on description—*fire and longing and wit*—of a major part of Dylan's appeal to many of his fans. Chabon was, of course, responding personally by invoking his birthday and his initial writing aspirations. At the same time, he was blending the personal with the critical to create his own discerning work, just as Roy Kelly had done at the *Telegraph* and various fans have done over the years and across the fanzines, journals, mass publications, and blogs of Dylan Town.

Michael Gray's *The Bob Dylan Encyclopedia* (along with its companion blog, which Gray posted regularly from 2006 to 2012) is the closest thing we have to a town record. Encyclopedist-with-a-sense-of-humor that he is, Gray even gives himself a third-person entry therein. For "Gray, Michael [1946-]" he wrote, "He wrote the first full-length critical study of Dylan's work, the pioneering . . . *Song & Dance Man: The Art of Bob Dylan*."[85] Now in its third incarnation, the nine-hundred-page work's "two strengths," as its author puts it, "are felt to lie in the critical assessments of individual songs and the depth of research into Dylan's sources."[86] Where the *Encyclopedia* is the entertaining and clearly opinionated town record of not only Dylan and the many who have influenced or been influenced by him, *Song & Dance Man III* has twenty rich chapters ranging from "Dylan and the Literary Tradition" to "The Coming of the Slow Train" to "Even Post-Structuralists Oughta Have the Pre-War Blues" (a 112-page chapter) and concluding with "There Is Only Up Wing an' Down Wing." Several of those pages have more footnotes than text, and the footnotes not only give musicological credit where credit is due but also often open out into mini-essays on topics ranging from fairy tales[87] to the place of trains in American roots music,[88] just to mention two of dozens of instances. It's a scholar's dream, clearly growing out of and exploding his self-described "rather Leavisite"[89] literary studies training and inclinations.

Gray's breathtaking knowledge of Dylan is the stuff of Dylan fan legend, as Kurt Gegenhuber reported on his blog *The Celestial Monochord: Journal of the Institute for Astrophysics and the Hillbilly Blues*. On October 1, 2010, Gegenhuber reported on attending a Bob Dylan Symposium in Minneapolis and then making the day trip to Dylan's hometown of Hibbing. It so happened that Gray shared the bus ride to Hibbing's open-pit iron ore mine and other significant Dylan sites. Gegenhuber stated, "Recognizing a once-in-lifetime opportunity, I turned to Michael Gray and asked the obvious question: Who threw the glass in the street?"[90]

This is only "obvious" to Dylan fans who recall the hotel scene in D. A. Pennebaker's *Dont Look Back*, a documentary about Dylan's 1965 British tour, and Dylan's persistent, heated questioning of the people in his hotel room about a mid-party incident. Where a fan like me would take pride in recognizing the reference and viewing it as a koan—"a rhetorical question and a bit of a joke— after all, the answer represents the quintessentially unknowable cipher that is the object of all Dylanology," as Gegenhuber put it—"Gray actually knew the answer, and offered a couple minutes of historiography contextualizing both the answer and the question itself." Beyond that, Gegenhuber described Gray as "generous with his time and knowledge, [a person who] listened closely, laughed easily, gave useful advice when I asked for it, remembered my name."[91] This should come as no surprise when we remember that Gray was there from almost the beginning at the *Telegraph* with John Bauldie and "Roy Kelly, an old Bobcompadre," as he described him on his blog in 2007.

I saw the same generous knowledge on display a few years later when Gray lectured at The University of Texas at Austin about Dylan and the blues. He was in complete control of his material and delivery and, by extension, his au- dience. As he autographed my copy of *The Bob Dylan Encyclopedia* afterward, he patiently made the case that I was mishearing a line about a cabin in Utah, rainbow trout, and children in Dylan's "Sign in the Window." I heard him, but could not convince myself to see it from his point of view.

The only other critic who might have as much Dylan information at his fin- gertips and off the top of his head is Clinton Heylin, whom Gray describes as "the Dylan biographer who started from the position of fan and collector" and became "a dominant figure in the world of Dylan fanzines and Dylan trainspot- ting."[92] According to Gray, "He has unearthed so much of the information we have about Dylan's recordings and his life, and has interpreted that information so forcefully, that had Heylin never interested himself in these subjects, the whole face of Dylanology would be different."[93] He then adds, "It would also be less combative."

In *Bob Dylan: A Life in Stolen Moments, Day by Day: 1941–1995*; *Bootleg*; *Bob Dylan: Behind the Shades*; *Bob Dylan: The Recording Sessions, 1960–1994*; *Revolu- tion in the Air: The Songs of Bob Dylan, 1957–1973*; and *Still on the Road: The Songs of Bob Dylan, 1974–2006*, Heylin set out to document Dylan's every moment and, increasingly in recent years, to interpret those moments. *Stolen Moments* offers, for example, that it was on February 14, 1961, that Dylan composed "Song to Woody" and that on September 9, 1990, he included a rare "Just Like Tom Thumb's Blues" in his concert at Palmer Auditorium in Austin, Texas. Some of the combativeness that Gray alluded to appeared in *The Recording Sessions*, in which, for example, Heylin described Mark Lewisohn's writing about the

Beatles as "staggeringly ignorant."[94] He even played up his combativeness in the acknowledgments to *Still on the Road*, beginning a sentence with, "Oh, and just in case anyone thinks I'm mellowing with age . . . ."[95]

Gray does not call Heylin a Bobcompadre and observes that his "achievement as a Dylan researcher and biographer is such that his notorious belittling of, and quarreling with, almost everyone else in the field is as unnecessary as it is crass."[96] This dustup in Dylan Town suggests one more dimension of good fandom and bad fandom, which concerns how fans relate to one another. Fans who want too much from their idols are one kind of monster. Those who feel the need to belittle fellow fans who either know less or disagree with them can quickly become another, regardless of how brilliant and prolific they may be.

Ellen Willis, the first popular music critic for *The New Yorker*, wrote "Rock, Etc." from 1968 to 1975 and blazed some trails without inflicting any collateral damage. She discussed fandom in general and Dylan in particular in a personal-critical style that kept interweaving her feelings, the music, and politics. As early as 1969 she wrote of fans and stated, "It's my theory that rock and roll happens between fans and stars, rather than between listeners and musicians—that you have to be a screaming teenager, at least in your heart, to know what's going on."[97] Without missing a beat, she then made the theoretical personal and admitted that she "grooved much more easily with records than with concerts," which was one more reason [she] "defected to folk music."[98] Her interest in Dylan and his fans preceded her years at *The New Yorker*. She wrote a fifteen-page article for *Cheetah*, a short-lived contemporary of *Rolling Stone*, in 1967 and it caught the eye of *New Yorker* editor William Shawn.

Shawn and other readers picked up on how Willis described Dylan and pointed to his decidedly literary bent. "A voluntary refugee from middle-class life, more aesthete than activist," as she put it in *Cheetah*, "he had less in common with the left than with literary rebels—Blake, Whitman, Rimbaud, Crane, Ginsberg."[99] Every few years she would check in on and write about Dylan. When *Nashville Skyline* was released in 1969, she heard that "[h]is attitude toward women, like his attitude toward everything else, has softened considerably. [It] is an album of tender, humor-filled love songs—not a putdown in the lot."[100] Five years later, she praised *Blood on the Tracks* for its open-endedness, stating, "Eventually, the marriage ends or survives, and he learns something about himself or he doesn't. . . . [H]e makes us see in his dilemma our own unreasonable yearnings, punctured illusions, furious defenses, painful accommodations."[101]

When she favorably compared Springsteen's relationship to his fans with Dylan's to his devotees, she did what Chabon would do decades later. That is, she wrote of both herself and much more. She returned to the territory of her earlier observations about fans and stars and hypothesized that Springsteen initially imitated Dylan because of "the obsessive way so many young men identified with Dylan during the middle sixties." She then parenthetically added, "(Not that women weren't influenced by Dylan, but the relationship was of necessity more oblique.)" before closing with "what Dylan represented—the possibilities of surviving a crazy system."[102]

Four decades later, Alex Ross was writing about music for *The New Yorker*, and both Dylan and fandom were still in the air and on the magazine's pages. In "I Saw the Light," Ross described leaving a Dylan show in Minneapolis and looking out onto the street and seeing what turned out to be the silhouette of Lyle Lovett's hair. Upon mistaking that hair for Dylan's and thinking that he might meet Dylan, Ross surprised himself with how excited he became and then reflected, "This episode pointed up for me the embarrassment of fandom. I hadn't requested an interview with Dylan, but for a moment I thought I was about to see him up close. I felt the bubbling excitement of a fan." That excitement led him to ask a significant question that he left unanswered in that article: "Is fandom as foolish as it feels?"[103]

Although I am reticent to use the word *foolish* about others without acknowledging my own openness to such a charge, two blogs did take Dylan fandom pretty far for my taste. They are the politically motivated *RightWingBob*, posted by Sean Curnyn, and *Radioactive Dylan* by Bryan Styble.

RightWingBob has appeared for the past ten years and considers Dylan from "another side," as Curnyn chooses to put it. His primary aim is "to challenge the persistent fallacies regarding the Left's ownership of Bob Dylan and his work."[104] This sounds fair enough, given that Dylan has always pretty much kept his politics to himself. But many of Curnyn's interpretations of Dylan, beginning with Curnyn's initial statement of principles about (as far as he was concerned) wrongly rejected Supreme Court nominee Robert Bork, underscore the dilemma of making one's own meaning of open-ended texts. Although each of us is certainly entitled to our own opinions, I am not convinced that, as Curnyn argues, "Red River Shore" is about the Holy Spirit. Not all reader responses are going to resonate as being true to the texts.

Another fan who takes great liberty with Dylan's work is Bryan Styble, who "founded and edited the early Dylan fanzine *Bob Zimmerman Blues*,"[105] wrote a fifty-six-page blog entry he titled "Like a Rolling Tombstone—Huh? . . . no WAY! I don't even GET stoned anymore!"[106] Based on the conceit that Dylan had died, it appeared in paragraphs of many colors and varied fonts. Anecdotes and Dylan-related puns ran all through it, including the notion of "the never-ending paragraph." Although Styble is clearly incredibly knowledgeable and undeniably energetic, the distinction that Michael Gray made between "critics and interpreters of Dylan"[107] kept coming to mind. As Gray put it, "The critic's function is a large and porous topic but 'Dylan interpreter' is a much narrower, clearer term and a far less useful creature, whose mutton-headed aim is to say what Dylan's songs are 'about.'"[108]

We know that Dylan did not think Paul Williams was mutton-headed. In fact, he apparently had his secretary order 114 copies of Williams's "Dylan—What Happened?" and invited Williams and his wife, Sachiko, backstage after four of his 1980 shows. According to Williams, Dylan even read him the lyrics of a then-new song called "Every Grain of Sand."[109] I return every few years to Williams's words about Dylan's conversion to Christianity in 1979. It is one of the great examples of fan labor as thoughtful, thorough, and generous criticism. Every discerning Dylan fan should have a copy.

Williams made his readers' time with him worth their while because he stayed close to the texts, which were Dylan's lyrics, and the public pieces of Dylan's private life to try to answer how Dylan could "walk out on stage and sing seventeen songs every one of which makes reference to and centers around the singer's special relationship with Jesus Christ."[110] It was vintage Williams, the writer and fan who strived to be in conversation with fellow fans. Williams began in a conversational spirit and with his eye sharply on Dylan: "What happened to Dylan, anyway? I'll tell you what I know, what I think, what I feel. I'll tell you the story as best I can piece it together." Then he gave his readers room to decide. "After that, you're on your own."[111] After thirty pages of looking closely at the albums of the previous ten years, Williams stated:

> What I think happened to Dylan is this: he came to New York an ambitious kid, made the scene, wrote some songs, made some records, became famous, kept on going and did a whole lot of great work and got so famous so fast with so many expectations from all sides that finally it blew up in his face, and through some kind of saving grace there was a woman there to save him, protect him, allow him to go on with his life.[112]

This was consistent with Williams's descriptions of the importance of both women and spiritual questions throughout Dylan's art. He based his persuasive claims on close readings of the lyrics rather than on journalistic speculation.

Then he concluded by looking back at the sixteen years of Dylan performances he had seen. He assured his readers that

> He's still the same person. He has the same strengths and weaknesses. He may have some new ways of handling those strengths and weaknesses, new truths, new insights, new methods of keeping himself in balance. New friends, new lovers, new shelter. But the same personality, same DNA, same voice, same heart and soul.[113]

Before sending us off on our own, Williams closed with the most generous words someone listening with a gentle heart in 1979 could possibly write: "Dylan does his work extremely well, and I love him for it. I must argue with him about the importance of pronouncing the Lord's name in a particular way, but that's all right. I admire his courage. I wish him Godspeed."[114]

A kindred intelligence and generosity can be found at *Gardener Is Gone: All Art Aspires to the Condition of Bob Dylan*, the blog of Nina Goss. As well as blogging about Dylan, Goss has published three volumes of *Montague Street*, a fanzine not interested in "reiterations of media coverage, announcements of upcoming projects, or reviews of bootlegs or current concert tours." Nor did "speculation regarding Dylan's private life" interest the editor. Instead the focus was to be upon "his artistry. . . . Bob Dylan's singing, songwriting, musicianship, filmmaking, painting, poetry, prose, radio-show hosting, and any currently unforeseeable endeavors."[115] The result, so far, has been a widely varied group of lively minds coming together around Dylan's art. William Carpenter's essay about "re-purposing" Dylan appeared in one issue. Professors, poets, musicians, and independent scholars have contributed to theme-based issues on Dylan-in-Time and Time-in-Dylan, the theme of confinement, and the 1989 album *Oh Mercy*. "Brownsville Girl," the song that Dylan and Sam Shepard cowrote, got a close reading in its pages and *Masked and Anonymous*, Dylan's most recent film project, received extensive analysis as well.

The wide variety of topics related to and spawned by Dylan's art can be seen in almost any of Goss's posts. For example, "As Each New Season's Dawn Awaits" of January 21, 2011, brings together the essays of Montaigne, the nature of the blogosphere, and Dylan's song "Tell Ol' Bill." Goss quoted Sarah Bakewell's claim in *How to Live* that Montaigne "invented . . . writing about oneself to create a mirror in which other people recognize their own humanity" and then followed up with her response, one that suggested another angle on the dilemma of who ends up with who at the table of joy. Goss wrote, "The problem being that one person's invitation to enjoy the companionship of an amiable, curious, and informed inner life is another person's desultory narcissism. . . . The lesson is that some people's restless rambles create a far more worthwhile *shared festival of humanity* [as Blakewell put it in *How to Live or A Life of Montaigne*] than others." At this point Goss connected Dylan's "Tell Ol' Bill" with Frost's "Stopping by the Woods on a Snowy Evening" before concluding, "Bob Dylan sings that *secret thoughts are hard to bear*, and we make a grave mistake to take this to mean he is unburdening his secrets to us. He shows us what the burden feels like, that's all he does and why ask for something else?" She then told her readers, "Limning our solitudes with the richest palette is not the same as relentless confession." Once again, what starts out to be about Dylan turns out to be about so much more, about the "shared festival of humanity" and the richness of the palette.

Something akin to Goss's allusion to Dylan's "secrets" runs through much of the best criticism not only of Dylan but also of fandom. During those Rolling Thunder days, Sam Shepard thought about some of those secrets and observed, "if a mystery is never solved, the case is dropped. In this case, in the case of Dylan, the mystery is never solved, so the case keeps on. It keeps coming up again. Over and over the years. Who is this character anyway?"[116] The question arises yet again: Why and how is Dylan different from other subjects of fan attention?

Greil Marcus, "a major figure"[117] in both cultural studies and Dylan criticism, has been diving into mysteries for decades. One of the pioneers of rock criticism, he began writing about Dylan in December 1968 in the *San Francisco Express Times*. He has been writing columns, reviews, and articles as well as a dozen books—*The Old, Weird America: The World of Bob Dylan's Basement Tapes*[118] and *Like a Rolling Stone: Bob Dylan at the Crossroads*[119] among them—ever since. He first saw Dylan perform in the summer of 1963, in a field in New Jersey, and described himself as an early "fan."[120] He even went so far as to write, "Along with a lot of other things, becoming a Bob Dylan fan made me a writer."[121]

He wrote a blurb about *Highway 61 Revisited* for "Treasure Island," the epilogue to a volume in which he gathered, introduced, and appended the contributions of twenty rock critics about their favorite albums. In that anthology, *Stranded: Rock and Roll for a Desert Island*,[122] he described Dylan's album in these words:

Like a rolling stone, if a Minnesota Isaiah calling down the spirits of Hank Williams and Robert Johnson could be a Rolling Stone. This was an explosion of vision and humor that forever changed rock, and a piece of music that stands as its signal accomplishment. It was also a journey through America (with a stop at a Mexican border town and a destination beyond the law), a map of its traps and glories.[123]

Marcus also wrote one of the most notoriously famous sentences in the history of rock criticism. In response to Dylan's 1970 album *Self Portrait*, he began his *Rolling Stone* review with "What is this shit?"[124] In a free-flowing format, he ended with a concern that expanded upon and clarified the opening sentence: "In a real way, Dylan is trading on the treasure of myth, fame, and awe he gathered in '65 and '66. In mythical terms, he doesn't have to do good, because he had done good. One wonders, in mythical terms of course, how long he can get away with it."[125] Over the course of the review, Marcus suggested that Dylan had fallen out of the company of Robert Johnson, Herman Melville, Hank Williams, Nathaniel Hawthorne, Mark Twain, Jimmie Rodgers, and John Wayne—an eclectic and characteristically Marcusian pantheon—because he lacked "the determination to follow up" his "vocation."[126]

Over forty years later, he wrote the liner notes for *Another Self Portrait*, as Dylan titled the tenth volume of his Bootleg Series. His words appeared between photographs of Dylan as the Woodstock country gentleman with short hair and a wispy beard. In some of the photos there are chickens in the yard and sandals on Dylan's feet.

Marcus quoted himself without comment and then went in another direction. What he now heard were alternate versions of the old tracks in different ways: "With 'In Search of Little Sadie' and 'Copper Kettle' as signposts, *Another Self Portrait* opens up as new territory: roads shooting in all directions, he stated."[127] He ended his second look at a very different *Self Portrait* by answering a Dylan riddle with a riddle and homage of his own. He riffed on the moment in Dylan's 1965 interview with Nora Ephron and Susan Edmiston when Dylan said,

"I've never written anything hard to understand, not in my head anyway … an' nothing so far out as some of the old songs. They were out of sight." Like what, Ephron or Edmiston asks. "'Little Brown Dog,' Dylan says. 'I bought a brown dog, its face is all gray. Now I'm going to Turkey flying on my bottle.'"[128]

Marcus then concluded, "That is here as 'Tattle O'Day' . . . something that fell by the wayside, and so weightless and free it might be the magic carpet that the little brown dog takes to get to where it wants to go."[129]

It is a terrific image but also open to an observation that Gray made about Marcus's "great technique." He described such moments as "writing [that] seems to pluck these verdicts from the air—verdicts with all the cryptic power of a guru up a pole, so that the hapless reader feels he can argue with neither the supreme self-confidence of the delivery nor with the content, since this is as ungraspable as it is forcefully done."[130] It is a comment about how Marcus sometimes writes, but it is also one about what Dylan brings out in so many of his fans. Dylan's language, music, and elusiveness invite such conversations because it all keeps nudging us to make clear what is in our heads and hearts.

Luc Sante gave it a try when he wrote, "Dylan is a mystery, as he has been since his first record. . . . Dylan is a complex, mercurial human being of astounding gifts, whose purposes are usually ambiguous, frequently elusive, and sometimes downright unguessable."[131] He added,

> At the same time he is a sort of communicating vessel, open to currents that run up and down the ages quite outside the confines of the popular culture of any given period. That he is able to tune his radio to those long waves in a time of increasingly short memories and ever more rapid fashion cycles is not the least of his achievements.[132]

That sounds like a pretty good answer to a question that I see running through much of the commentary of Dylan fans. I include myself as one of those fans trying to figure it all out.

In Dylan Town we're all listening, and sometimes calling in, to "his radio." On the best days, when the reception is clear, we can hear not only those "long waves" but also the many voices responding to him. Then some of Emerson's words ring true: "Life is good only when it is magical and musical, a perfect timing and consent. . . . You must hear the bird's song."[133] On such days, when the reception is clear and the wind is blowing just right and the first stars promise a perfect night, I can hear not only the bird's song but also *the crickets talking back and forth in rhyme* all across Dylan Town. Those are pretty good days and very sweet nights indeed.

CHAPTER TWO

Teaching Dylan

In the words of Dylan, *it all began on a long-forgotten morn.* Or at least the official teaching part did. In the spring of 1999 I turned in a request to list "English 524: Dylan" for the fall semester at Southwestern University, the liberal arts college in Georgetown, Texas, where I had been a faculty member since the mid-Eighties. I hoped that the course would be approved by the curricular powers that were and, once it was listed, that there would be enough student interest for the course. For years I had been weaving Dylan moments into my classes, frequently including "Mr. Tambourine Man" in survey courses, even though it was not in the anthology, and occasionally working *Dont Look Back* onto my "Sixties Hollywood" syllabus as "an example of an anti-Hollywood movie." I would justify doing so by stating, "It's important to look at works outside the mainstream in order to see that stream more clearly." Then I, and most of the students, would enjoy the hell out of director D. A. Pennebaker's 1967 black-and-white film of Dylan's 1965 United Kingdom tour, the one the year before they called him Judas.

We would watch the young Dylan, in his mid-twenties and every bit as cocky as then heavyweight champion Muhammad Ali, take down his British counterpart Donovan with a mesmerizing "It's All Over Now, Baby Blue." Dylan's performance in the noisy, crowded London hotel room that suddenly fell silent as he sang *The empty-handed painter from your streets / Is drawing patterns on your sheets. . . . The carpet, too, is moving under you* made it very clear that although he and Donovan may have been in the same room, they were not on the same planet in terms of what or how they sang. Donovan's rhymes were of the "moon-June" school that most songwriters of the time favored and that Dylan derided during interviews. Dylan's lyrics were paintings with words, movies set to music, unlikely rhymes of protracted vowels and quirky juxtapositions. It all added up to how remarkably smart, confident, and charismatic Dylan was in his early twenties. Students shook their heads that, in 1965, Dylan had been only a few years older than they were as they watched him on film. Year after year, without fail, they were transfixed. (The only other surefire moments from what students called "back in the day" were the Beatles' final rooftop concert at Apple Records and Michael Jackson's first moonwalk in 1983. The students' responses to those performances proved that a few magical performers occasionally transcend time and cross historical space.)

Showing *Dont Look Back* also provided an opportunity to play a bit with the title. I suggested that Dylan must have gone along with Pennebaker on it, including its dropped apostrophe, given Dylan's fondness for breaking as many formal rules as possible in his liner notes during that point in his career. "They might have been having some fun," I stated, "with both the myth of Orpheus and baseball player Satchel Paige's words 'Don't look back. Something might be gaining on you.' Or maybe it was just a reference to a line in Dylan's song 'She Belongs to Me.' Whatever the title referred to, they were clearly messing with the more conventional types, which was almost everyone else, around them." I offered this in the spirit not of cracking some code but rather of suggesting how much Dylan, or any other richly allusive writer, might bring out in his audience members if they are willing to play along. In fact, I made certain that I tempered my claim by reminding them, "Part of the movie is about Dylan taking on people who read too much into his work." More than once he told his listeners to decide for themselves what they thought, which is exactly what I urged students to do with whatever they were studying. "All the same," I then added, "how great is it that three words can turn us into cultural magpies weaving together mythology, baseball, a Dylan song, and the rules of punctuation?" The students who enjoyed the movie always seemed to like the question. They were beginning to have some fun and to see the joy of making a few connections between Dylan's words and their worlds.

When I made my proposal to my department chair I did so knowing that I had probably never taught three consecutive class sessions, regardless of the subject, without alluding to, quoting from, or digressing about Dylan. He was not the only writer I knew or cared about, but he was the one I knew and cared about the most. I did not think his songs held all the answers, but I loved the way those songs raised so many questions and nudged me to come up with my own answers. He drew on so much of American cultural history, and his words just kept appearing—on the radio, in print, in conversation, at parties I went to, in my head. He was, among other things, one of my best teachers. So, when one observant student visited my office that year and pointed out that the pictures of Dylan on my walls and desk were quite a bit larger and slightly more numerous than those of my wife and children, I said, somewhat sheepishly, "I've been with him longer."

During my pitch for awarding students credit to study Dylan, I pointed out that the Stanford Humanities Center had just convened its 1998 International Conference and "devoted *all* of it to Dylan and his work." The italics were those of the organizers, and I italicized the word *international* as I shared the conference description with my department chair. I highlighted some particularly resonant buzz phrases: "one of the most important—and enigmatic—popular artists of the twentieth century . . . an international icon and talismanic figure for several generations . . . the multifaceted nature of his art and his cultural legacy . . . an interdisciplinary context." I may have invoked our opportunity to be "cutting edge and out in front of Dylan Studies," in part because I had recently read Don DeLillo's *White Noise* in which such language is used. I knew that DeLillo was satirizing "cutting edge" as the last refuge to which a self-perceived pedagogical expeditionary clings. But I could not resist the temptation, and I played my ace when I asserted, "The students have been clamoring for a semester devoted primarily to Dylan." I was proud of using the word "primarily," which came to me in an inspired moment that would give those of us who thought about course enrollments some wiggle room. When the course was approved, I began hoping for the flood of student interest that I had promised so that I would not be proven wrong the first time I used *clamoring* in a professional context.

When thirty-two students, a healthy number for an English course at our school, signed up during preregistration, I shifted my fretting about whether another generation found Dylan talismanic to whether I would have enough material to play, hear, read, and discuss over the course of an entire semester. As anyone who really knew their Dylan lyrics, history, and criticism would have told me, there was *no reason to get excited.* The riches were embarrassing, even then.

Over the subsequent fifteen years those riches have grown exponentially, and I have taught numerous versions of "Dylan" to various populations. I have incorporated Dylan into my version of the department capstone for graduating English majors, created a first-year seminar devoted to his work, and led a three-week Free School class for any of the university's employees interested in taking it. Each time the course has come up in the departmental rotation, there has been yet more music, art, and commentary to bring to the party. Although I didn't see it working out this way, "Dylan" is starting to feel like the Neverending Class.

My first time was in a converted dorm room with an overhead projector bolted to the ceiling. I brought an extension cord to plug my boom box into the wall. I also carried a coffee table book, Jonathan Cott's 1985 *Dylan* for Rolling Stone Press, and a few magazines to pass around so students could see some of Dylan's many looks over the years. Across those pages and over those years there was Dylan at Newport in 1964, when he was conducting a workshop under a billowing black-and-white canopy and, to my way of thinking, looking like the coolest person on the planet in his jeans, boots, and jacket. They checked him out with the Rolling Thunder Revue in 1975, when his face was painted white and he was at his most theatrical, performing "Isis." There were photos of him cracking a whip in a motel parking lot, diving into a swimming pool, riding a motorcycle near Woodstock, rolling a tire down an urban street, and, very often, smoking a cigarette. By showing these pictures and having students read what was being written about Dylan "then rather than now," I wanted to add another layer to their (and, yes, my) senses of different historical moments and Dylan's responses to them. I also was fascinated by the magic I associated with so many of the pictures and hoped that if the students didn't exactly share my particular fascination with Dylan that they might nonetheless be encouraged to think about their own interests. I wanted them to know that, as was the case with Dylan's influences and subjects, there was room for almost anything under the metaphorical tent we were pitching in that classroom.

Some of the students looked at the pictures as if they were Matthew Brady's record of the Civil War or Walker Evans's portraits of Alabama sharecroppers in *Let Us Now Praise Famous Men*. Dylan in the Sixties, and even in the Nineties, was clearly that far removed from most of their lives. But now and then a few lingered on a particular page before nodding and smiling like they were looking at a colorful uncle they had heard tales about at family reunions or some space alien from one of their half-remembered dreams. "Did anyone else have hair like that back then?" they would ask. "What was with his fingernails?" occasionally came up. One or two had seen some of these pictures before, thanks to their parents, older brothers and sisters, or a friend. Several students liked that he had the courage to be "alternative" with that hair and those fingernails. They commented that his "attitude" leaped off the pages. "I guess he was always a gangster," one of them said in a way that suggested it was the ultimate compliment a 1999 student could pay a 1964 character. I loved the comparison and responded by quoting enthusiastically from "Isis": *"Well, I guess."* Having heard the song the first day of class, they caught my drift.

When the music played, everyone tapped their feet to the bouncier tunes like "Silvio" and "Black Diamond Bay." Someone said that "Lily, Rosemary, and the Jack of Hearts" would work at a square dance, and everyone immediately heard how wonderfully strange "Brownsville Girl" was with such lines as *The only thing we knew for sure about* Henry Porter *was that his real name wasn't Henry Porter* and *"We're going all the way 'til the wheels fall off and burn / 'Til the sun peels the paint and the seat covers fade and the water moccasin dies."* One day I even heard a student call a classmate Henry Porter and viewed it as both a nod to Dylan and a moment of what I would learn to recognize as "repurposing." A few people quietly sang along or moved their lips to "Blowin' in the Wind" and "Mr. Tambourine Man" as the words came out of my paint-splattered speakers. One wrote a reflection about how Dylan's line *jewels and binoculars hang from the head of a mule* fascinated her when she heard it on her parents' stereo at the age of six and "was beginning to try to figure out who my parents and their friends really were." Many of the students had similar recollections of hearing "that voice" at family parties or by swimming pools. We were, I realized, entering the lands of recovered memories and new frontiers. They were two of my favorite places.

At one point during that first semester, I joked about the nuts and bolts of the course with my departmental pal Debby Ellis by way of a passage in Claude Levi-Strauss's *Tristes Tropiques*.[1] I had been saving the passage for just the right moment ever since graduate school, when I first read it and it struck me as wonderfully cinematic in a *Raiders of the Lost Ark* kind of way. Finally, that moment had arrived. When he described attending the lectures of fellow anthropologists in Paris, Levi-Strauss gave me some texture for the movie that was in my head: "The projector, which was fitted with inadequate bulbs, threw faint images onto an overlarge screen, and the lecturer, however closely he peered, could hardly discern their outlines, while for the public they were scarcely distinguishable from the damp stains on the wall."[2] The inadequate bulbs, overlarge screen, and damp stains all connected me to Levi-Strauss who, I told myself, was not only the world's greatest anthropologist but also must have been around my age at that time in his life. Like me, he was an academic starting his teaching career with high hopes, stories to tell, faulty equipment, and small audiences. Although it hardly needs saying, I was thinking big.

"Our protagonist," I told Debby that morning before I had even put my books and papers down, "is using a sound system that comes across like late-night AM radio on a road trip through the Midwest. Close your eyes and you can hear that crackling signal, the one that keeps breaking up. He is some kind of latter-day, well, Levi-Strauss. Instead of returning from the Amazon rain forest, though, he is bringing back reports of Dylan in the Sixties. Maybe we could get [Robert] Redford to play him in his later, successful life. He could be looking back at Brad Pitt playing him as a young, dashing teacher with an amazing head of hair. We'll call it *Tristes Tropiques Redux* just to see if we can get that one past the studio guys and pull in the academic crowd. It's gonna be a helluva story."

Debby, a medievalist by training who once told me that I was "the crazy younger brother [she] never had," looked puzzled but not totally displeased by my latest idea. She smiled and said that she had to get ready for her Chaucer class. I saw something in her eyes that made me think of Redford's line to Paul Newman in *Butch Cassidy and the Sundance Kid.* "You just keep thinkin', Butch. That's what you're good at" was in her eyes as she went prepared to talk about "The Pardoner's Tale."

As it turned out, we never made that movie. On the other hand, I no longer lug my boom box and extension cord into a funky classroom with a jerry-rigged sound system. In fact, I am now but one of many professors on various campuses teaching Dylan courses. Because our university has prospered, and not just because of my Dylan courses, I have more technology than I know how to use. I have learned how to get my movies and photographs of Dylan on perfectly sized screens in rooms with sound systems that I can turn up pretty loud, which is sometimes necessary to do justice to the volume that Dylan wanted during that 1966 tour.

For me, the story of Dylan in the classrooms is a feel-good one. The literary canon has become somewhat larger and more fun. Although it would not be accurate to say that the entire professoriat has embraced Dylan Studies or that students are clamoring more than ever for more Dylan, he is still iconic and talismanic enough to fill a class at our school every few semesters. He also continues to be an ever-richer text for interdisciplinary study, as evidenced by the growing number of publications about him and conferences at which Dylan scholars and fans come together. I would never say I told anyone so, but I have frequently entertained the thought that the folks at Stanford in 1998 were on to something and that I was only a few steps behind them.

This minor sea change has been very good for me professionally and personally. I delivered a paper about Dylan and Springsteen at "Glory Days: A Bruce Springsteen Symposium" in New Jersey in 2005 and an Ignite Talk of twenty slides in five minutes about the connections between Dylan, Bing Crosby, and the nuclear polka band Brave Combo at the Experience Music Project Pop Conference in Seattle in 2013. Over the years in between I talked about Dylan in New York, Boston, Monterey, and San Antonio. Each time I learned a little more about him and a lot more about his fans, which, in turn, has been inseparable from the way I think and go about my teaching. I have made some new friends and had more than my share of epiphanies during my Dylan travels. I owe him and his fans a lot.

In Jersey, right there in Bruce's hometown, I puckishly argued that Dylan's *John Wesley Harding*, which Springsteen cited as an inspiration for *Nebraska*, was superior to Springsteen's album because of Dylan's wordplay and calm. My small but engaged audience was evenly divided between students from Monmouth University and faculty from around the world. Most of the latter group were wearing variations on early Springsteen—jeans, T-shirts, and leather jackets. A few, like me, wore ties but had their shirtsleeves rolled up. Everyone knew quite a bit about Dylan and, unlike me, seemingly everything about Springsteen. They unanimously disagreed with my assertion. The Europeans were particularly disappointed in what they took to be my lack of appreciation of Springsteen's "dark authenticity," as one of them described it. "You just want him to keep doing *Born to Run*, don't you?" he said with a sad shake of his head.

Another panel participant, a young second-year professor from Germany, told me, "With all respect, I have to say that you are typically American in how much you dislike anything that looks like pessimism."

I said, "I hear you, but I want the wordplay and an occasional moment of light. And is there any song on *Nebraska* that comes close to 'The Ballad of Frankie Lee and Judas Priest' for being so much fun about things so serious?"

We talked a bit longer, trading specific lyrics and agreeing about the pared-down effects on the two albums. I liked the irony of the albums' respective backstories: that an alleged loner like Dylan would head over to the house they called Big Pink to jam with the Band in the late Sixties while the usually extroverted Springsteen went into his garage alone in the wake of Reagan's election. It was fun to know these facts because they took us into the different narratives we had woven from them. During those brief conversations we were citizens of the republic of music. We were sharing and comparing fans' notes.

I came back from New Jersey, as I did from every good conference, with a new perspective. I also had connected with a few more kindred spirits who wore their musical passions on their sleeves, rolled up and otherwise. Being with them nudged me to articulate why, as much as I liked Springsteen's music, politics, and generosity onstage, I was even more drawn to Dylan's language and style. In such moments I had to walk some of my classroom talk about how "it's not good enough to say 'I just like it better.'" I had to identify, articulate, and then own my preference for wordplay and humor over leanness and pessimism. Doing so made me more aware of and comfortable with what I wanted students to do.

In Seattle, eight years later, the Pop Conference that I attended met in a museum funded by Microsoft money, designed by Frank Gehry, and centered upon Jimi Hendrix, who is to Seattle and the Experience Music Project what Springsteen is to New Jersey and its shore. The EMP is a space with not only the auditorium in which we presented our Ignite Talks but also sound labs, meeting rooms, and ongoing exhibits. Hendrix's 1967 jackets from London were behind glass, just like the Gutenberg Bible at the Humanities Research Center in Austin or Leonardo's *Mona Lisa* at the Louvre. There were music journalists and interested Seattle residents as well as university professors in attendance. I liked the blend because it struck me as appropriate to a gathering about popular, as distinguished from academic, culture. Much of what I heard was presented in the language of writers who write for general audiences. It was my kind of crowd.

My kind of music, Americana, was but one of many genres on a program with far more about hip-hop and electronica than about folk. Most attendees wore bulky black sweaters between their name tags and their rain gear. I spoke at breakneck speed about the place of Christmas albums in American popular culture ("huge"), Mitch Miller's clout at Columbia Records ("significant") and his lack of enthusiasm for Dylan's music ("intense"), Dylan's recasting ("sincere") of the Christmas songs of his childhood, and his shout-out ("liner notes") to Brave Combo for their version of "Must Be Santa." I was sandwiched between a presentation about Yoko Ono's shape-shifting and one on the Seattle rave scene, both of which struck me as better prepared, delivered, and received than mine. I knew that I was taking a chance with Christmas music and fifteen seconds a slide. That format collided with my loose and baggy nature. But I had told my students that semester, "It's good to make yourself think and write outside your comfort zone." I also knew that it was good to perform outside my comfort zone because it reminded me how important performance is to teaching. I felt justified harping away about "Dylan taking risks" by taking a small one myself. It was hardly my moment of going electric at Newport, but it was a small step and one that I shared with my students. It was important for them to hear and see that I was still a work in progress, just as I told them they and every artist we studied were.

I returned to the conference the following year, more to listen than to present, and felt like I was at home. John Shaw, a Seattle writer who had spoken about Woody Guthrie on the same panel that I had spoken about Christmas music, remembered me and my talk. A large, easygoing man with a great smile, he was gracious and told me, "You made me think about Dylan in a different way." He then asked, "How is your project coming along?"

"I'm running a bit behind, but going to make it," I said, sounding as confident as I could.

He smiled warmly and told me "absolutely" in a way that somehow reassured me and made me feel that someone had not only listened, but also reached out to me.

I also talked with Daniel Cavicchi about his work on Springsteen, Peter Coviello about his Steely Dan article for *The Believer,* and Kevin Dettmar about editing *The Cambridge Companion to Bob Dylan.* I listened to their presentations and panels, made note of the way Dylan popped up throughout the conference (one songwriter said she had spent some of her early career copying Dylan's lyrics just to see them on the page in her own writing), and heard nothing that threw a major wrench in where I was headed regarding Dylan's significance. The hardly surprising through line was that he continues to be a touchstone to many musicians and music writers.

At the last session I attended, Greil Marcus was speaking about his history of "Like a Rolling Stone." In response to a question about how he kept writing when he was not sure of his direction, he paused briefly and then said, "You just have to tell the story." I knew what he meant and it made the conference for me. Feeling like a kid in a candy store, I told Norma, "They are all in my bibliography. I 'just have to tell the story.'"

I didn't always feel like a kid in a candy store, much less one with a story to tell. Although many of my contemporaries in graduate school were already wise to the ways of the academic and literary worlds, I was a slow learner. Being part of larger conversations was not really on my radar when I applied to graduate school or, for that matter, during my first few semesters of study. The research and writing that I did for my classes was, at best, uneven. I was drawn to graduate school by my love of reading and the possibility of teaching. I applied, got accepted, and went because—after a year in law school, weekends at a rental car business, a summer of serious misadventures in Sheetrocking, and another six months of shelving books in the Collections Deposit Library where I was third (of the library's three employees) in command—I realized how much I missed my undergraduate English classes. I wanted to live what I had heard some people describe as "a life of the mind."

For me, this meant finding a way to learn and to teach and, perhaps someday, to write about what I most cared about at the time—music and movies and baseball and my friends. I wanted to enjoy long meals around various tables of joy. The way I saw it, there should always be music in the air. Jewels and binoculars might hang from the head of a mule. I had seen a lot of people in movies and a few professors in life live that way, and I had heard Graham Nash sing his generational anthem about the ideal hippie house with cats in the yard. I suspected that I had a better chance of living that kind of life as a college teacher than as a lawyer, rental car clerk, Sheetrocker, or sub-sub-librarian. I knew a life of the mind was possible no matter what one did because I had already met some very fulfilled and thoughtful attorneys, rental car clerks, Sheetrockers, and librarians. I just wanted to enjoy what I was doing more than I enjoyed reading about civil procedure or parking Ryder trucks or using a nail gun or creating convoluted games about which book would end up on which shelf when I had emptied my book truck. What I really wanted to do, like so many college graduates, was to keep living the better parts of the life I lived in college. I wanted to start teaching like a few of my favorite teachers, in and out of school. I wanted to keep on keeping on and repay some of the good deeds that people had done for me.

To claim that my kind of thinking fit right in at The University of Texas at Austin's English program in 1975 would be a bit of a stretch. Most of my fellow graduate students, although they also wanted lives of the mind, were immersed in literary theory, comparative literature, and conspicuously working harder than everyone around them. I, on the other hand, preferred to read contemporary fiction and slick magazines, go to the movies and watch baseball games, hear music, and make up for all that time I was nowhere near being cool. I also wanted to bring some of what I took to be Dylan's attitude and style into what I did and how I lived. I would occasionally say something like "*the sun's not yellow it's chicken*" just to see if anyone would go along with me. Once in a blue moon someone did. They, too, usually didn't exactly fit in and, more often than not, we became friends.

To complicate matters further, I had become much more serious about cooking than I was about studying a second language, which was a requirement if I was to go on beyond the master's to the PhD program in English. I started reading cookbooks, in English, and seeking out recipes that took at least an hour to prepare and called for a particular spice or an exotic mushroom that took the better part of an afternoon to locate. It was good, honest escapism, but escapism nonetheless. One night, as I waited for a sixty-four-ounce bottle of vegetable oil to come to a vigorous boil for a Chicken Kiev recipe, I almost blew up our two-car garage apartment. In response to that evening of the instant cinder, I educated myself about temperature-control frying pans in a way that I never educated myself about the sonnet form. I then bought myself a unit and mastered the recipe in time to prepare the dish for twenty people who attended a friend's wedding rehearsal dinner. The evening was the high point of my first semester and, that being the case, spoke a thin volume to me about the road I was on.

The more I thought about the manifold meanings of the Kiev Incident, the more I started getting those old law school, Sheetrocker, rental clerk, and sub-sub-librarian *déjà vu* blues. I was, once more, in danger of drifting too far from the shore, as the old gospel lyric had it. Although I was grading some papers, giving an occasional lecture on Frank Lloyd Wright's architecture or the Black Sox scandal of 1919, and being mentored for my very own class if and when the opportunity arose, it wasn't all that I had hoped it would be.

In large part, this was because I was basically an apprentice in a strange guild and getting distracted by my fellow apprentices. I spent too much time imagining how they were faring with our professors and too little time actually reading about the sonnet form or Puritan poetry or Samson's agonistes. The more I imagined others currying favor and reaping rewards, the more off the collective beat I felt. I had a recurring dream in which I played the role of Mickey Mouse in Disney's *The Sorcerer's Apprentice*. What the dream lacked in originality it made up for in angst. I started to wonder if I would ever get through the program, much less get a teaching job. Dylan's *Blood on the Tracks* and Joni's *Court and Spark* were my albums of that moment. Both were filled with tales of relationships that had gone wrong told in beautiful, heartbreaking lyrics. I played them as I cooked and felt their lines becoming my lines. I started a list of great opening lyrics from all my albums and decided that it was impossible to top Bob's *Early one morning the sun was shinin' / I was layin' in bed.* I listened and cooked and waited to get my own classes. As I did so, I told myself that I was a bit like a squirrel storing food for the winter. I decided not to share this image with anyone.

The differences between me and my fellow graduate students were never more pronounced than on the first of the month, when we all got paid for our teaching assistantships. I learned that most of my cohorts either trusted the United States Postal Service to deliver their checks or used this relatively new innovation called direct deposit because, as one of them asked me, "Who really has the time to wait in line for a check?" I, for one, had the time if it meant avoiding getting my money a few days late due to some HAL-9000 computer glitch right out of *2001: A Space Odyssey.* I had recently heard Jack Nicholson's J. J. Gittes say, "Sometimes I take all afternoon for lunch" and modified the approach to fit my paydays.

I started payday in the basement of The University of Texas tower, where I would wait with the groundskeepers, physical plant workers, and custodians who got a kick out of my clogs and long hair. Some called me *huerco* (kid) while others preferred *flaco* (skinny). We took turns bringing in a dozen breakfast tacos from Hector's Taco Flats and waiting for our checks. They told me about their families, vacations, and some clubs on the east side. Now and then we played a quick game of dominoes. When they asked me what I did for the university, I told them I was "teaching a book about a whale." The next month I said the book was about a kid who got kicked out of prep school. Their favorite was about the guy who was living underground with 1,369 lightbulbs and eating vanilla ice cream topped with sloe gin. "Ah, *huerco*," they said, just shaking their heads.

As soon as I got my $378 check I deposited $353 of it at a Travis Bank and Trust branch across the street from the Tower. I would then begin the process of buying a novel from the Vintage Contemporaries series at Garner and Smith Books on the Drag. I did so only after an hour of religiously browsing all the shelves, reading passages from the various contenders, and petting Gus the cat, whose station was right beside the cash register. Shortly before noon and the arrival of the lunch crowd, I would make my way to an outdoor table at a coffee shop called Les Amis and order a piece of hot apple pie with cheddar cheese and vanilla ice cream because that's what Kerouac's Sal Paradise did when he was on the road. I would nurse my cup of coffee and wade into the first pages of my newly acquired novel by Tom McGuane or Steve Erickson or Richard Ford or Ann Beattie or whoever editor Gary Fisketjon and the crew at Vintage had anointed that month. Sometimes I would mix things up a little and begin with

The New Yorker or *The Voice Literary Supplement*, if either had hit the stands that day. Now and then I saw some of my fellow graduate students walking by alone, with their heads down, or in intense conversation with one another. Occasionally I saw one of them walking by with his (it was always *his* in these particular cases) head down and in intense conversation with himself. Every few months one of my professors would pass by on his (it was always *his* in those days) way to the faculty club with a group of chuckling colleagues.

I went undetected in plain sight, an academic version of *Mister Roberts*'s Ensign Pulver, the Jack Lemmon character who the ship's captain had never seen over the course of Pulver's two years as laundry officer. I was Poe's purloined letter, hidden right there in plain sight. I actually liked it that way because, as I knew from reading Ralph Ellison in one of my favorite undergraduate classes, "[i]t is sometimes advantageous to be unseen."[3] As I drank my coffee, put down my reading of the moment, and reflected on Ellison, I wondered if Dylan was possibly thinking about him in "Like a Rolling Stone" when he sang *You're invisible now, you got no secrets to conceal*. I liked thinking that was possibly the case, and I got a kick out of pulling up the end of that stanza on my inner turntable. I was having fun connecting some dots on a puzzle that was all my own and that I might eventually make good enough to share. In such moments, Les Amis was both my laboratory and my meditation space, just as a whale ship was Ishmael's Harvard and his Yale. I was not out to prove anything about Dylan or anyone else because, as I told myself each time I counted down to the Varsity's first feature of the day, the fun was in the making rather than in the proving.

Dylan's lyrics, which I had heard for years, were starting to take on a richer meaning to me in a way that made me think again of Ellison, who wrote, "Who knows but that, on the lower frequencies, I speak for you?"[4] I had shared that sentence with some students and told them, "Bob Dylan speaks for me more than anyone else I have ever read or heard." I then asked them, "Who speaks for you?" I got all kinds of answers—The Clash, a hometown minister, Allen Ginsberg, a grandparent, Jesus, their high school coach. I listened and asked them to write about why that was the case. I told them that "Like a Rolling Stone" was a new song every time I heard it and that so much of what I had listened to before I had never really heard. "Listening to Dylan I feel like Melville when he first read Hawthorne," I told them. "I feel like I'm starting to grow and see no end in sight." Such thoughts came to me more readily in a café than in the library and more easily with students than with my classmates or professors, which is part of why I kept going to Les Amis and why I kept looking forward to teaching my own classes.

After mopping up the melted vanilla ice cream with my pie crust crumbs, I would spend my remaining $5 on the Varsity's double feature that afternoon. It did not matter what was playing there because whatever it was—a science fiction pairing of the original *Invasion of the Body Snatchers* and the 1978 remake; two classic westerns; both *Godfathers* (*I* and *II*, that is)—was terrific. I would walk the half block east on 24th Street beneath Carlos Lowry's mural of famous film stills. Looking up at images of Orson Welles delivering a speech in *Citizen Kane*, James Dean sitting in his car in *Giant*, Cary Grant running from a crop duster in *North by Northwest*, Claudette Colbert wearing Clark Gable's pajamas in *It Happened One Night*, I made my way to the front door of the theater on the corner of 24th and Guadalupe. The glass door had a sign that simply said "NO ALIEN JUNK FOOD," a phrase that I found elegant in its directness and rich in its connotations. To me, it was almost a haiku. I daydreamed about someday working those four words into my first book or maybe even using them for the title of a short story about two moviegoers, one a thinly disguised stand-in for me and the other the woman of my dreams, on converging paths toward the movie that would begin their complicated romance.

One windy October afternoon, while I was finishing up at Les Amis, a woman who was beautiful in my favorite hip kind of way—thrift-shop scarf, faded jeans ripped at the knees, boots—walked by and turned the corner at the Varsity. She had terrific red hair and was, I told myself, Leonard Cohen's "lady of the harbor" from "Suzanne," fallen to earth on a sidewalk in Austin. I tried to figure out a way to ask her about tea and oranges all the way from China. We both went into *Stop Making Sense*, Jonathan Demme's documentary of a Talking Heads concert, and then our respective ways, without exchanging a word.

What I most remember from that day, besides seeing her, is that on the big screen in the big suit and with the sound blasting out of the speakers, David Byrne was amazing fronting the band. The percussionists and backup singers had all forty of us in the Varsity dancing in front of our seats. So, in a roundabout way, the lady from the harbor and I did dance together one afternoon in the gloaming. It was too loud to ask about the tea and oranges, but I told myself it would be our unspoken thing. The excitement of the crowd was palpable in the lobby and out on the early evening street. We were putting our hands to our foreheads and kept repeating the same four words we had just heard Byrne sing in "Once in a Lifetime." At that moment we were all connected, and I loved it.

Fortunately, a few of my professors understood that my gifts were more social than analytical. By example and during our conversations over the years, they showed me ways of teaching and helped me see how I might become my own kind of professor. They urged me to focus upon what I really cared about and reminded me to keep looking forward to my first classes because, as they told me in their very different ways, I had something to teach. I needed to hear that more than I realized or liked to admit.

The first of those professors was Bill Stephenson, whose "British Romanticism" class kept me from leaving graduate school that first year. I took it when my other classes, and the whole graduate school culture for that matter, did not suit me any better than being in law school, hanging Sheetrock, renting cars, or shelving books. I immediately liked Stephenson because he didn't really look like he fit in that culture either. He reminded me of Richard Brautigan on the cover of *Trout Fishing in America* more than he did of the rest of the people in the halls, and it quickly became apparent that he had much more interest in Wordsworth and Blake than in peer-reviewed publications and university politics. He viewed his students as individuals with their own stories to tell rather than as potential research assistants.

Because he was so easygoing and never stoked the competitive fires that seemed to be burning all around us, I summoned the courage to ask him if I could mash up what little I understood of Thomas Carlyle's novel *Sartor Resartus*, its term "the Everlasting No," and Joni Mitchell's song "The Last Time I Saw Richard" for my final paper. I admitted that my approach was "a bit journalistic and slick," particularly for a class in which everyone else was writing about mimesis, the anxiety of influence, or the mirror and the lamp. I said that I wanted to suggest that, at least in those two works, Carlyle and Joni shared a related notion: that we all go through and, if we are blessed, move beyond hard times. I was as taken with Mitchell's album *Blue*, on which "The Last Time I Saw Richard" appeared, as Stephenson was with Blake's *Songs of Innocence and Experience*.

He tugged at his mustache, furrowed his brow, and then told me, "Why not? It's a bit strange, but I like it. You should have some fun writing and will no doubt teach me something. I look forward to reading it." His words were my first license to play.

As I put Carlyle's Teufelsdrockh, who had written a treatise on clothes, in conversation with Joni's characters, who were listening to a Wurlitzer in a Detroit bar in 1968, I felt that accelerated heartbeat I had been missing. It took me back to pulling all-nighters to write papers on my electric typewriter to the accompaniment of James Taylor's *Mud Slide Slim and the Blue Horizon* because that's what an English major on the way to becoming an American novelist did. When Stephenson publicly praised my paper for "making connections" and spent some time on Joni's line about a guy in a bar going through a bad patch, I had trouble hiding my pride. On the way home from school that day my step was both lighter and quicker.

In that paper, which I called "Dark Café Days," I was doing something akin to what Dylan and so many folk artists had done when they drew upon what came before them and made a new version of it their own. Twenty-five years later, I found these words from Dylan in *Chronicles Volume One*: "Opportunities may come along for you to convert something—something that exists into something that didn't yet."[5] Although intellectual property lawyers split hairs over what constitutes conversion, I like to think that Stephenson and I got the spirit of Dylan's words long before he wrote them.

Bill Stott of the American Studies program also urged me to pursue what interested me. Stott wrote an Oxford University Press book about documentary expression and Thirties America that was praised by Hilton Kramer in the *New York Times*. The *Times Literary Supplement* called Stott "the Aristotle of documentary." In a department of intellectual historians, he went his own way—"kind of like a different kind of Dylan," I told a few of my buddies—and taught Pauline Kael and Joan Didion ("Two popular journalists, for God's sake!" snorted the program's early twentieth-century intellectual historian). One of Stott's seminars, "Great Bad Books," was devoted to pulp fiction and self-help manuals. He noticed the color of Gene Kelly's socks in *An American in Paris* because, he told us, "Such details matter." He taught *Tristes Tropiques* through a literary lens, Roland Barthes's *Mythologies* as "one more type of cultural reportage," and Clifford Geertz's "thick description" as a stylistic technique rather than an anthropological approach. He was a meticulous editor of our papers and a difficult reader to please. Because he showed me what kind of subject matter might make its way into the classroom and had infinite patience with my writing, Stott helped me not just to stay in school but actually find my path through and beyond it.

He always preferred simple, direct prose and was particularly fond of certain voices like Kael's and Studs Terkel's. Because Stott was naturally shy, he celebrated and even seemed to envy people as comfortable in their own skins as Kael and Terkel appeared to be. He put them before us to encourage us to be both feisty, like Kael, and generous, like Terkel, in whatever we undertook. Like Stephenson, he had a broad sense of what we should read, discuss, teach, and write about. His classes never seemed to be only about the texts we were reading. They were, I told my friends who were not in graduate school, "about life," as I shared something we had read for Stott or talked about how I wanted to do what he did when I grew up.

He assigned Kael's "Trash, Art, and the Movies," in which we read, "If we've grown up at the movies we know that good work is continuous with not the academic, respectable tradition but with the glimpses of something good in trash, but we want the subversive gesture carried to the domain of discovery."[6] Seeing these words at a time when I was figuring out my relationship to "the academic, respectable tradition" hit home. Celebrating "the subversive gesture" in pop culture was something I liked the sound of, even if I did not totally understand all its possible manifestations. I heard something akin to what Kael was saying in Dylan's music and words. It was the same "something" I liked about Ali's persona, Jack Nicholson's acting, Springsteen's songs, and the New York Yankees of the late Seventies. It was something that I could share with the students I was starting to work with in "American Studies 355—Main Currents in American Culture." I was beginning to see some light in the tunnel.

The light grew brighter when I studied with Warwick P. Wadlington, whom everyone called Wick. He taught nineteenth- and twentieth-century American literature and specialized in Melville. Around the time I took a course from him, he had turned his interest in Melville's phrase "godly gamesomeness" into an article about play and tricksters. For me, the phrase was the key to Wick's style. It also described the kind of teacher I wanted to be. I had never seen anyone bring so much joy into a classroom. He helped me see the greatness of Melville's wild and lively interest in absolutely everything and, moreover, why so many American writers (Dylan among them, as I later came to realize by way of his references to *Moby-Dick* in at least three different songs) thought so highly of his 1851 masterpiece. He showed us that *Moby-Dick* was "the book as world" and frequently emphasized that we should not miss Melville's sense of humor along the way. The second point was particularly important to me because all too few of our professors ever acknowledged the place of humor in literature or life.

Wick also listened when I told him about what I was reading, like Toni Morrison's *Song of Solomon* or Maxine Hong Kingston's *The Woman Warrior*. He then followed up with me after reading the books himself. In so doing, he reminded me of a basic human courtesy. He showed me how to contend with the occupational hazard of being too much in my own head, and I took it as my responsibility to follow my friends' trails as much as possible. After all, that was one of the points, a collateral joy, of a life of the mind.

Although I had guides and spirits along the way, I still had much to learn. I had appreciated the Romantics enough to know that I was jumping in far from fully formed. My first classes were only nominally my own. I was responsible for the lectures and the grades, held weekly office hours, and doubled my monthly income. All of that was in my hands, but I was still assigning the canonical texts I had been assigned as a student. I loved my Dylan, Ali, Springsteen, Yankees, and movies at the Varsity but viewed them as guilty pleasures rather than the serious stuff of the profession. As much as I appreciated the encouragement I had received, I knew which way the economic wind blew. Among my favorite professors, only Stott taught popular culture. He did not start out teaching "Great Bad Books," and I saw how doing so made him an outlier with his colleagues.

Like the professors who ran most English departments in most North American research universities, UT's professors worked on their individual research projects with graduate students in their field and plugged rookies like me into large-enrollment, heavy-lifting, non-sexy, tellingly called service courses like "Rhetoric and Composition" until we worked our ways up to level-two service courses like "Survey of Literature." That was the system, just like farm team baseball. When I broke into the game in the late Seventies, very few insiders were openly questioning it. Teaching Dylan was, at most, a very dimly flickering light on an incredibly distant horizon. If I said I'd been planning it for years I'd be lying. Part of the story that I am telling is how that came to happen. As I hope is becoming clear, that story is, in almost equal parts, about how some of the academic world moved toward Dylan and how I moved through a part of that world.

I started out on the first floor of Parlin Hall, only a few doors from the department chair's office, with twenty freshmen students taking "Survey of American Literature" on a late Tuesday afternoon in the fall of 1978. My briefcase was a day old and light brown. I was wearing a coat and tie, dressed like I thought a young professor should dress (more Gregory Peck in *To Kill a Mockingbird* than Stephenson, Stott, or Wadlington). Once I got going, I took off my coat, just as I had planned the night before. I was filling the blackboard with information I had gathered regarding Sylvia Plath's "Daddy," making my case almost as much about the poem as about my own blazing intelligence. I had information about Plath's brief and painful life, the confessional poem, a few of her contemporaries. The chalk was flying, and I was in my own wonderful little world. I would read a line or two to the rapt students, tell them what the lines meant, turn my back, and write yet more illuminating information on the board as chalk flakes faintly fell onto my blue shirt, white shrapnel from my hieroglyphs about Plath's husband Ted Hughes or her summer internship in New York. I was on a mission and in a trance. As we moved toward the poem's angry and chilling last stanza, and my grand finale, I began worrying about how little time remained to get it all on the board. I just had too much to say, just knew too much, and noticed that a few students were writing it all down as fast as they could. "By the end of the semester," I told myself with as much humility as I could muster, "they will be writing it all down. Like Updike's wife did when she heard Nabokov at Cornell."

Then, a nanosecond after my self-congratulatory note to myself, the classroom door flew open, and I saw the vapor trail of a student who had been sitting in the second row. She was a blur of long brown hair, orange T-shirt, shorts, tanned legs, and sandals as the door closed behind her. I hesitated for a moment and then felt like there was nothing to do but dismiss the class a few minutes early. The dramatic conclusion I was moving toward, when I would quote Plath's *I'm through* just as the bell rang, was replaced by shuffling feet. No one stayed to ask me what "Daddy" or what had just happened meant. I briefly wondered if the students were really taking notes about what I was saying or were, perhaps, instead writing letters to their friends back home or finishing a paper for another class.

I still remember the student and wish that I had apologized to her for my insensitivity. It was a rookie mistake compounded by serious delusions of grandeur. I have now been in and out of classrooms long enough to know what I should have known on day one: that we all carry all kinds of things into any room on any given day. Her exit may have had nothing to do with "Daddy" or with me. It could have been about her roommate or some bad food at lunch just as much as it might have been about her family life or her dislike of Plath's use of the word *bastard* or the cut of my jib. Whatever the reason she left, she returned to the next class and to almost all the rest of our meetings that semester. We never discussed the incident because the appropriate moment to do so had passed.

I did, however, change one aspect of my teaching the next time we met and every day thereafter. I abandoned my elaborate chalk masterpieces for typed outlines that had the major points I hoped to make and the passages that I hoped we would discuss. I handed them out at the beginning of class and made sure that I watched how students were reacting to the material and to one another rather than imagining how amazing I was in the role I had created for myself as a soliloquizing dervish in a cloud of chalk. Putting our chairs in a circle or around a table helped. Even better was meeting outside. I quickly got rid of my jacket and, later, my tie. That day reminded me of a couple of things that I sensed but had lost track of: just as students carried ideas about themselves, I carried plenty about myself, and I had a lot to learn about not only their ideas but also about my own.

My sense of self wasn't all that I carried into my first years of teaching. I also accepted the party line and the reward system that was attached to it about who belonged in the anthologies, like Sylvia Plath, and who did not, like Bob Dylan. That was even more of a weight for me than my interest in style. One could dress a lot of different ways, sending the signals best suited to the purpose of the moment. A professor could be incredibly cool or atrociously unfashionable. In academia, even rock musicians were welcome, as long as they taught and wrote about the traditionally celebrated works of playwrights, poets, and novelists who were valued for their complexity and timelessness.

Sterling Morrison, who had been a guitarist with The Velvet Underground before he came to Austin, was a case in point. His office was in the basement of Calhoun Hall, two floors below mine, where he worked on his committee-approved dissertation about the four signed poems of Cynewulf. He looked liked Ichabod Crane in a turtleneck. He also smoked a lot of cigarettes with Marvin Williams and Laurie Sledd. The three of them had arrived in Austin a few years before me and quickly took me under their wings, telling me, "We know that you can see through a lot of the bullshit." I took it as a compliment.

We had our doubts about the department's ruling class, but—and this is the important point—not about its canon or syllabi. Regardless of how we outsiders felt, we all assigned Chaucer and Shakespeare and Dickens and Faulkner and Plath. We might allude to Lou Reed and Leonard Cohen and Bob Dylan and Joni Mitchell during a class period. But they were not on our syllabi, in our anthologies, or sold in the University Co-op. We shared really terrific or incredibly funny things our students had written, commiserated about our workloads compared to those of the senior faculty, drank a few beers, and, most frequently, trashed "the chair and his minions," as we called them from our basement bunker. In our eyes, they were, at best, stodgy and, at worst, duplicitous. I invoked Dylan, describing us as pawns in their game. We smoked another cigarette and kept teaching the canon. Sometimes we hung out with a tenured linguist who was deeply frustrated with the way the department was ignoring its responsibility to writing instruction.

Sterling used up his teaching time before he completed his dissertation and went to Houston to become a master mariner and, eventually, a tugboat captain. Laurie left school and moved to California. I lost track of Marvin, although the last I heard he was teaching in Waco. The linguist fumed on. Even when it was going on, it all felt too much like the last lines of "Tangled Up in Blue," which had just been released: *Some are mathematicians / Some are carpenters' wives / Don't know how it all got started / I don't know what they're doing with their lives.*

I moved from English to American Studies, both to avoid taking a second language and because I saw Stott doing some of the things I wanted to do but could not do in the English Department. In American Studies, I did eventually teach Kael as well as Roger Angell on baseball. I put movies like *Citizen Kane* and *The Searchers* on my syllabi. I found ways to talk more about Dylan. I completed my dissertation on Americans in Paris after World War II. It was more journalistic than scholarly and cleverly titled "The Sun Also Sets." For reasons I always understood, it did not appeal to publishers. I returned to the English Department as an adjunct, back in the "service courses" trenches, where I was what Melville might describe as "a Loose-Fish and a Fast-Fish, too."[7] I taught, wrote, and worked on my kitchen skills.

It was definitely a couple of steps up from my life as a graduate student. No PhD orals or dissertation defense loomed. Even though I had over one hundred students, there were multiple paydays throughout the month and more hours at the Varsity. Inexpensive music played all over town every night. I was a contributing editor for a monthly magazine called *Third Coast.* Continental Airlines had sent me to Madison Square Garden to cover Patrick Ewing's first game with the Knicks. I went to the British Open to complete a story about Austin golfers Ben Crenshaw and Tom Kite. We had seen Dylan perform a few times during those years and not been disappointed, even if the *Street Legal* show was "a bit too Las Vegas" for most of my fellow fans. I parted company with them on that one and was just happy to see Bob, from however far away. He looked like he was having a good time, almost dancing. I loved the brass and the backup singers, and I knew even then that there was something special about the way they sang "Changing of the Guards."

Then one spring afternoon in 1983, in the early days of my postdoctoral life, the Dr. Pepper machine in Calhoun Hall was empty, and I took the next major fork in the road. Unwilling to forego my beverage, I went to the adjoining building, good old Parlin Hall, for my D.P. Right above my backup machine, tucked in among the advertisements for apartments and notice of books for sale, was a typed flyer reading "ADJUNCT WRITING FACULTY, SOUTHWESTERN UNIVERSITY, GEORGETOWN, TEXAS, 512-863-6511." In retrospect, it was a moment akin to Steve Martin's stopping for the talking road sign in *L.A. Story*. It turned out to be the point on which I pivoted into the next part of my story.

Interviews for the position were ending that week, and I decided to call on a whim more than out of any real career-building plan. It really didn't make much sense because I was already teaching four classes a semester, editing movie reviews, writing occasional feature articles that got me free plane tickets, and always running behind. I'm not really sure what I was thinking other than that I might like to make a little bit of extra money. One other thing that was far in the back of my mind was that I was an incurable pushover for anything that looked like it might be turned into a good story, particularly one about serendipity.

The department interviewed me to teach two sections of first-year writing. I liked the people in the room because they talked most about their students. The pretension quotient was low. There was a palpable difference, in emphasis and collegiality, between this English Department and the maze that I had been on the edges of at UT. The entire department was in five individual offices on one floor. It was day and night compared to UT's two buildings and one hundred adjuncts. In fact, the UT English Department alone had more part-time employees than the entire Southwestern tenured and tenure-track faculty. In Georgetown, when I first interviewed, there were no basements or minions or cautionary tales that jumped out at me.

I talked about my freelancing as much as I did about my teaching and mentioned that my wife, Marie, a city planner, and I were remodeling a hundred-year-old house in Austin's historic Clarksville neighborhood. I told a few jokes and discussed Melville and Dylan. As I left the interview, I felt that the department members were entertained and I probably would not get the job.

I did not know that an unsolicited letter on my behalf had come a few days before from John Ruszkiewicz, a Rhetoric professor at UT, who had heard of my teaching through the departmental grapevine. Years later I would learn that the letter, coupled with the interview, had persuaded the department to recommend me to the provost for part-time employment in the fall. Not one to turn my back on serendipity, I took the job and, like many other adjunct faculty members, I stacked my schedule with Monday-Wednesday-Friday classes on one campus and Tuesday-Thursday ones on another. And so I joined the "commuter faculty," a rapidly growing species in a marketplace glutted with PhDs and thin on retirees.

I taught first-year writing, as did everyone in the department at Southwestern. My students were baseball players and theater majors and first-generation students who were excited to be in school. They all knew one another in ways I had not seen among students in Austin, and many of their professors, me included, were mentors to them. I liked the closer connection with students, the lack of a graduate program, the small department.

Almost a year to the day after I started my part-time employment at Southwestern, 102 of 107 postdoctoral faculty at UT were "released" because the department voted to abolish a number of undergraduate requirements rather than to risk a class-action suit for de facto tenure. I was one of the 102. Those who foresaw the restructuring, the tenured linguist among them, were angered because it confirmed their notions about cynicism and duplicity at the top. Those who did not, and particularly my fellow adjuncts, were in various states of shock and panic. I, thanks to an empty vending machine and a letter from an angel I hardly knew, had been one step ahead of the flood.

A few years earlier, Wick had spent some time on what became one of my favorite passages, a moment from "The Mat-Maker" that I never tired of reading and sharing. Ishmael, coming out of one of his dreamy moments and concluding yet another of his terrific extended analogies, pronounced, "[A]ye, chance, free will, and necessity—no wise incompatible—all interweavingly working together ... chance by turns rules either, and has the last featuring blow at events."[8] The working together of the empty D.P. machine, the Ruszkiewicz letter, and the Parlin 102—no wise incompatible—made me feel like living proof of Melville's worldview. I also found myself singing, but only to myself, Dylan's line from "Idiot Wind"—*I can't help it if I'm lucky.* I knew it was bad karma to sing it aloud while those with a different kind of luck were trying to figure out their next steps.

Time passed. Many of the Parlin 102 left academia. Through various simple twists of fate, I kept winning the lottery and went from adjunct instructor to tenured faculty member to department chair to program director. I still taught canonical American writers, but in a canon that was rapidly changing to include previously excluded writers. Several of them were even the writers I had read at

Les Amis on my paydays *in another lifetime.* Lo and behold, Donald Barthelme and Ann Beattie and Raymond Carver had made their ways into the anthologies! I also taught other courses—ones on travel literature or film or memoir. I was inching my way toward Dylan, gathering material and continuing to figure out how I really wanted to teach and what I thought served students best.

A few of my new friends at Southwestern appreciated my Dylan thing, just as my professors had understood my café-day ways. They shared my enthusiasm about Bob, in varying degrees, and we often found ourselves talking about or through Dylan. Daniel Castro, a historian by training and a Beat poet by disposition, frequently reminded me that *money doesn't talk it swears.* When I was getting a little bit too attached to a program I was directing, he appropriately warned me not to be a *little boy lost* [who] *takes himself so seriously.* That was but one of many examples of Daniel's gift for calling up the perfect Dylan line for whatever situation was before us, whether it was a project for taking computers to Honduras or a question about who would inherit my old couch. More than once he shrugged his shoulders and told me, *it's life and life only.* Political scientist and cultural omnivore Eric Selbin would occasionally slide a bootleg under my office door as well as steer me to various stories all across the Internet about Dylan. Whenever Dan Yoxall traveled on university business, he sent me postcards he had spotted along his way. One showed Dylan in front of City Lights with poets Allen Ginsberg, Lawrence Ferlinghetti, and Michael McClure. In another Dylan was sitting on a park bench in Washington Square. On each of them Dan wrote, "Dude: HE was here. So are we. Love, Dude." Our head football coach, Joe Austin, and I agreed to disagree on whether the line *Be careful not to touch the wall, there's a brand-new coat of paint* was a bridge on the way to a rhyme with *saint* or an in-joke for a lover or, perhaps, both. One day, Mark Miller, a screenwriter who visited with me every few months, quoted "Wedding Song" from *Planet Waves: What's lost is lost, we can't regain what went down in the flood / It's never been my duty to remake the world at large / Nor is it my intention to sound a battle charge.* He did so without missing a beat. Until that moment, our conversations about cult movies, the screenplay he was writing, or the courses I was teaching had been short and sweet. Mark's recitation, coming out of nowhere as it did and delivered perfectly, was like a scene in a Monty Python movie. The campus mailman, Tom Swift, knew all the words to Dylan's "Silvio." I occasionally overheard him singing it as he made his rounds. One particularly fine morning, when we no doubt had more important things to do, Debby Ellis and I spent ten minutes discussing the gender politics of "Brownsville Girl." We laughed through our close reading of *You always said people don't do what they believe in, they just do what's most convenient, then they repent / And I always said, "Hang on to me, baby, and let's hope that the roof stays on."* Before we let ourselves get too carried away, we also reminded one another that *let's hope that the roof stays on* was followed instantly by its backup singers' amazing howl in three-part harmony.

It was a short distance from the delight of such moments to part of what I wanted to happen in my classes. Because I hoped those classes would be ongoing conversations that had a direct bearing on what students were doing in their lives, my classroom style of 1978 was long gone with the wind. I still prepared outlines, but also asked more open-ended questions on tests and for papers. Eventually, I discovered that assigning the right kinds of oral reports, ones that linked the class work to work in another class or life outside of class, increased student interest and class participation. Whether the topic was an evolving American literary history that now included writers I had read at Les Amis or Hollywood movies that were no longer categorically dismissed by my colleagues as "trash," from the first day of class I strived to make it clear that the course was as much about how students responded to the subject matter as it was about the subject matter itself. I began the semester with a statement that I repeated often throughout the semester: "What you think is as important as what you have read, seen, and heard." I explicitly emphasized the connections between what artists had made and how the students wanted to live. This hardly made me unusual, particularly at a liberal arts college, where what we studied and its relationship to the world beyond the university was central to our articulated mission. I just happened to find that relationship richest and most accessible through contemporary writers, popular culture, and, of course, Dylan.

Judging by the work of some of the students over the past fifteen years, they did as well. In that first Dylan course, the one with the boom box and the coffee table books, I received the following response to the final paper assignment, which asked "Why Dylan?": "Why should my life serve as proof to Dylan's significance? All I can say is that Dylan has played a significant role in my life and this is the only way that I can really show you that." *This* turned out to be a free-verse autobiography that interwove recollections of growing up with Dylan's lyrics. The student went on to teach school in West Texas and wrote me that she brought song lyrics into her high school classes. A few years later a similar assignment resulted in "Life Lessons Taught by Bob Dylan." It began with an epigraph from an assigned selection by Paul Williams—his observation that "It's hard to be lukewarm about a hero figure"—and culminated in the student observing, "Few people have experienced as many bumps in the road as Dylan has on his epic journey, and he teaches us that it truly is 'life and life only.' Maybe one day I will be able to shrug off the rough spots, too, and keep wandering down the road uninterrupted." That same semester, another student wrote about going with her mother to see Dylan in concert in San Antonio and observed, "Maybe Bob's songs are bits and pieces of a dream home that he's trying to assemble. I could be wrong, but that's part of the beauty of Bob. He's given people the tools to construct whatever they might dream up." The more I read their papers, the more I realized that students were learning something new about themselves, their families, and their culture as they wrote about Dylan.

I particularly looked forward to the students' oral reports because I never knew what was coming and because it was good to see them sharing with and responding to one another. I liked their taking ownership of part of the class and the way the conversations rippled out and looped back. On those days class was much more like a lively town meeting than the lectures I sat through as an undergraduate. Students loved it when one of their classmates brought in his acoustic guitar and, with his hair constantly falling across his eyes, played Townes Van Zandt's "Kathleen" after giving us background information about *Another Side of Bob Dylan.* They requested, and got, an encore in an afternoon that turned into an impromptu coffeehouse. Another found Blind Willie McTell's "Broke Down Engine Blues" and had us listen to it to get an idea of what Dylan was responding to when he sang *nobody sings the blues like Blind Willie McTell.* She said it made Dylan's piano playing on the song "even more powerful." A report on "Boots of Spanish Leather" launched a many-sided conversation, one in which I was a mere bystander, about why breaking up was so hard to do.

In each instance, students were teaching one another and me about the music that influenced Dylan as well as about the music that he had influenced. Beyond that, however, they were also finding a way to talk about what really mattered to them, which was not necessarily Dylan but rather the roads they were on and the hopes that they had. Increasingly, they would bring in the work of their favorite artists, the people who mattered to them as much as Dylan mattered to me. In that spirit, the students in the first-year seminar made videos that used Dylan songs as jumping-off points for what they wanted to say about topics from religion to sexuality to drug use to being an international student in the United States.

When I taught a Free School class, in response to the call for "whatever you think you know something about and would enjoy sharing your knowledge with friends and colleagues," ten people I worked with signed up. We were between the ages of thirty and seventy and from various academic departments, the Business Office, the Physical Plant, the Library, and Development. There were no papers, presentations, or grades. We read *The Rough Guide to Bob Dylan* just to get the bare bones. Mostly we listened to music and talked for two hours once a week after work in May, about what we heard.

I liked the challenge of figuring out how to begin to talk about Dylan in such a compressed format and thought of it as trying to do something akin to producing my own double album or a four-chapter approach similar to David Yaffe's *Like a Complete Unknown*. Given that my fellow workers, just like the students over the years, knew anywhere from a lot to nothing about Dylan, I decided to let chronology be our way in, although it was a chronology heavily tilted to 1965–75. We briefly touched upon the highlights—the move to New York, going electric, the motorcycle accident, the divorce, being born again, the Never Ending Tour—but didn't dwell. Our time was spent more pleasurably and productively listening to and comparing notes on particular songs and turns of phrase. We did watch Dylan and Donovan, and it was no different for my coworkers than it was for the undergraduates. They were mesmerized.

I started making CDs for each class meeting so that we were not reading or talking about songs (or particular versions) that some people had not heard. Class members came in each week and, as per my only request, led the conversation about their favorite song of the previous week. The university's master carpenter questioned Dylan's sincerity about family in "Sign on the Window," stating that he doubted Dylan really believed a cabin in the woods and kids was what life was "all about." A librarian marveled at the Newport audience during Dylan's performance of "Mr. Tambourine Man." Our events planner talked about how hilarious "Isis" was. One person, who had seen drug problems among her friends, questioned Dylan singing *everybody must get stoned*. I never jumped in to break ties or speak as "an expert." For me, it was good enough to share the question with my Dylan friends.

The two hours passed in the blink of an eye. Dylan was once again right: *Time is a jet plane / It moves too fast*. There were a few converts by the end of the class, and we all knew one another a bit better. No one left doubting Dylan's genius. Norma and I still take those four CDs and the two codae I made on our road trips. Those selected 480 minutes of fifty years of work have yet to get old for us.

It wasn't until the fall after the Free School class that I came across the words that best expressed what I had been striving for over the years. I was preparing for the English capstone course on popular culture and Dylan. I had read various fan studies theorists and was particularly taken with the way Henry Jenkins wrote about textual poachers. The phrase had a nice ring to it. But I had yet to find exactly what I was looking for in terms of the alchemy that could happen when people shared and repurposed what they cared about the most.

Then one serendipitous payday, while browsing the stands at Book People, my current Garner and Smith, I found *The Believer*'s 2012 Music Issue, which contained Peter Coviello's "The Talk That Does Not Do Nothing." As he wrote about "the Dylanishness of [Steely Dan's] Donald Fagen's diction and phrasing," Coviello described one way of thinking about what we might do in our best moments of teaching and learning:

> It is what you do when you are young, but not only (I think) when you are young: you love things (songs, records, books) and in the abundance of that enthusiasm you talk, you measure that love with and against others'. You mix your words and your delight up with those of another person, or of many people, and you feel out what's provoking, or disquieting, or otherwise pleasing about how those words and those enthusiasms rub up against one another. What you forge together is a kind of idiolect, a semiprivate argot of appreciation and critique, ardor and invective.[9]

Coviello then described such conversations as "also, often, love songs."[10]

So, as I think about a future course offering, I'm torn between two Coviello-inspired titles that I like very much: "Love Songs" and "The Table of Joy." Both would open up what I want to explore next with students. Beyond that, all I really know is that Dylan will be one of the headliners. My hunch is that students would clamor for such a class.

CHAPTER THREE

My Back Pages

Of course, my particular Dylan story goes even further back than when I began imagining that I might teach a course devoted primarily to him. Like all of our individual stories, it begins with growing up, with what Holden Caulfield called "all that David Copperfield kind of crap."[1] Like Holden, I will spare you *all* of mine. That said, I still need to describe some of how, as I now see it, my father set me up to love Dylan and how, sure as the world kept turning, a few key events during my semi-wonder years nudged me even more in that direction. As I do so, I have no choice but to introduce some of my fellow travelers and acknowledge how they were tributaries into the River Dylan that has run through my life. I owe them that. It's also the only way to follow Greil Marcus's advice and tell the real story.

My father, Sidney Gaines, was described by the people in our town of Grand Prairie, Texas, as "very liberal" for a number of reasons. He had the *New York Times* and *New Republic* delivered to our house on Hill Street. He and civil engineer Lloyd Strange were the entire Great Books discussion group at the public library. Born Jewish, he liked kidding his fellow physicians at Methodist Hospital about taking donations for Guns for Israel or the American Civil Liberties Union (he was only half-kidding about the ACLU). When my brother Steve and I went on rounds with him, the doctors, nurses, and people who worked in the hospital coffee shop would smile and tell us, "Your dad is a character." The way they said it made it clear that *a character* was a good thing to be, even if they did not share his politics.

Back then, he was the only doctor in Grand Prairie who made house calls in Dalworth, the neighborhood in which African Americans lived, shopped, and went to segregated schools. After my father died, people told me some of their stories about him. I learned that he rarely charged his Dalworth patients and that he occasionally gave them money to buy clothes or a bed for one of their children. Before Steve and I were ten, he took us to pick cotton one hot summer afternoon because, as he put it, "I just want you to know how some people get by." He took off his suit coat, rolled up his white sleeves, loosened his tie, lit another Chesterfield, and sweated while he worked with us for an hour that felt like the entire day. Many years later, when I saw the photographs and footage of Dylan singing "Only a Pawn in Their Game" in Greenwood, Mississippi, in the summer of 1963, it struck me that Dylan and my father, in their particular ways and during those early days, were on the same side. It was the side I wanted to be on.

But sharing his politics with me was only part of how my father prepared me for an appreciation of Dylan. He also had a terrific sense of humor. For example, he never tired of telling us about a fellow medical student named Steven Panick. The entire reason for his shaggy dog story about Panick—a story that included information about Panick's hometown and his photographic memory and his eventual specialization in radiology—was to get to the punch line, to what the medical students always said to him: "Panick, you're a riot." The payoff always cracked us up, no matter how many times we heard it, because Fath—as Steve and I and our friends took to calling him once we were teenagers and wanted a name for him that was both casual and distinctive—so enjoyed delivering it. Part of Fath's being *a character* was his love of a good story and his fondness for a joke. This was no doubt one of the reasons people invariably smiled when he came into a room. For him, justice was the most cardinal of the four cardinal virtues and, if he had his way, he would have added humor as a fifth one.

Besides his decidedly liberal politics and his gift of laughter, Fath had definite aesthetic preferences that tilted heavily in a sentimental direction. One of his favorite stories was E. B. White's "The Second Tree from the Corner," which contained what he described as "the key sentence in life, Dave": 'What *do* you want?'"[2] He had no problem with, as he put it, "getting a little misty," be it over a *New Yorker* story that he loved or a song or movie that touched him. His displays of emotion resonated with me much earlier than did his, or anyone else's, sense of social responsibility or mastery of comic timing. I was probably wired, and definitely raised, to be a sentimental guy. There might be people out there who can claim "I was always hip," as John Lennon did in an interview in 1980.[3] I am not one of them. Instead, I was always sentimental. Only later, when I started listening to and looking at photographs of Dylan and the Beatles, did I want to be hip. My definition of the word allowed for a good amount of sentimentality.

The first music I remember hearing was at the Dallas summer musicals with my family. Fath and Mother would take us to Fair Park for dinner before a Broadway classic that was most frequently about young lovers whose stories always ended well. No opera, jazz, or country and western entered our young ears. The name Elvis sneaked into some conversations I overheard between the nurses in Fath's office, but it was Broadway hits and the Tin Pan Alley of the Gershwins and Cole Porter that played on our record player at home. I liked the stories of good people overcoming their initial romantic challenges, which were pretty minor in the grand scale of things, and living happily ever after, which appeared to be easy to do in Fifties America. I took it for granted that I would be one of those people someday, singing about the street where she lived or talking happy talk.

Most of the movies we watched covered similar territory and ended happily as well. Chaplin, and particularly *The Gold Rush* with its rags-to-riches plot, was Fath's favorite. He once sneaked his Minox camera (he called it "a spy camera" because of its size, silver verticality, and fast shutter) into a theater and took stills of Chaplin filleting his shoe for the prospectors' Thanksgiving dinner. Around that time, Fath told me, "Chaplin wrote the song 'Smile' for *Modern Times*. Imagine that!" We went to see the big-budget movies—*Around the World in 80 Days, Ben-Hur, Lawrence of Arabia, The Sound of Music*—on Sunday afternoons in Dallas and then headed to Goff's for chili cheeseburgers and cherry ice cream. All in all, it was good times.

For me, there was something even better than all of those musicals, movies, and songs, though. It was a category unto itself, one made up of nothing but Errol Flynn swashbucklers. *The Adventures of Robin Hood, The Sea Hawk,* and *Captain Blood* were the entire syllabus for the informal course in popular culture and personal style that Fath taught me. Flynn was my gateway to Dylan and, as it turned out, to so many of my other favorites. (Years after my introduction to Flynn, I could not help but smile when I heard Dylan conclude "You Changed My Life" with *You came in like the wind, like Errol Flynn* and learned that "Foot of Pride" contained a reference to *your fall-by-the sword love affair with Errol Flynn.*) Flynn would be the first person, the George Washington, on my own private and crowded Mount Rushmore. Dylan and Lennon would eventually join him, as would Nicholson's J. J. Gittes and Wes Anderson's Fantastic Mr. Fox. It's a Ruckus Rushmore, one that I see as a Red Grooms painting, made up of characters all cut from a similar cloth. They are good outlaws with definite attitudes and a variety of romantic streaks.

My love of those Flynn movies was no doubt enhanced by what a production Fath made of watching them. First of all, I got special dispensation on any night a Flynn swashbuckler was playing on television. Those nights Fath urged me to eat lightly at dinner because he would be making a rare kitchen appearance to "cook," as he insisted upon saying, his famous cottage cheese salad. Our ritual went like this: everyone except the two of us were in bed around 8:45; small-curd cottage cheese, tomatoes, cucumbers, green onions, bell peppers, and black pepper were on the kitchen counter at 8:50; two durable plastic bowls with dishwasher-faded rims sat right there beside the ingredients; chopping and assemblage, with running commentary from the chef, had been completed by 8:55; more cracked pepper was added; then we went to the couch in front of our black-and-white DuMont as the credits began to roll over the Erich Korngold score.

For Fath, Robin Hood, like Captain Peter Blood and Geoffrey Thorpe (which was the Sea Hawk's name before he was the Sea Hawk), embodied everything a hero was supposed to be and much of what I needed to know about the world. "He's taking up for the little guys," Fath would say as we watched Robin of Lock-sley, who was privileged and could have easily ignored the little guys, or Peter Blood, who was an Irish doctor with a missionary streak. We liked Korngold's rousing music that accompanied men jumping out of trees to ambush the Sher-iff of Nottingham's stooges or pirates swinging onto a ship to take it from the Spaniards. We never tired of the sword fights and particularly liked when they played out as shadows on castle walls or took place on a beach as the tide rolled in. Most of all, we enjoyed our mutual loathing of Flynn's frequent nemesis, Basil Rathbone. We worked his terrific name into conversations whenever we could. For us, *Rathbone* was code for a despicable character on the side of wrong, be he a Mississippi governor standing in a school doorway to block James Meredith or a local banker throwing his weight around with the school board. Whenever I said, "He's a regular Rathbone," Fath would pause before responding. More frequently than not he would state, "Perhaps. But he's definitely more to be pitied than censured." Fath was always more forgiving than I was.

These movies were great excuses for us to discuss not only good and bad guys but also underdogs. But before I fully appreciated such conversations, or even caught their drift, I was riveted by Flynn's style, his confidence bordering on arrogance. When he entered Nottingham, with his eye patch and hood, I realized that a hero could look like something other than a cowboy, a baseball player, or an astronaut. That was the moment that I slowly started moving toward heroes with longer hair, rascals who wore tunics and capes and knee-high boots, and had a mischievous twinkle in their piratical eyes. The combination clearly worked for Olivia de Havilland, who was both Flynn's recurrent love interest and my first screen crush. I liked that she could keep up with Flynn, but also eventually succumbed to his charms. And so, between bites of the best cottage cheese salad ever cooked, began my fascination with the dashing, good-hearted, and slightly rebellious ones.

Summer camp also contributed mightily to my preparation for Dylan. Every July between 1958 and 1964 Steve and I went to Friday Mountain Boys Camp outside of Austin. The camp—which was on land where Texas legends J. Frank Dobie, Walter Prescott Webb, and Roy Bedichek had spent time talking and writing about the Southwest—was owned and run by good progressive Democrats. The counselors were University of Texas undergraduates out of school for the summer. Given the time and the place, there were folkies as well as football players among them. We played and talked sports, went on nature hikes, and came into Austin for a day at Barton Springs, the spring-fed pool with sixty-eight-degree water that was and still is the best pool in the Western world. At night we sat around campfires and heard Buster Lewis, who had been in the Peace Corps, play his guitar. I learned "Stewball," "This Land Is Your Land," and "Blowin' in the Wind," a song that we all associated with Peter, Paul, and Mary at the time.

Captain Kidd, the camp owner and director, told stories both around the fire and from an old motel chair with peeling red paint out in the yard. Every year he told the one about Bristletop, who used to live in the main house and had eyes that looked out of his portrait directly at us no matter where we stood in the living room of that old stone house with the screen porch and the daddy longleg spiders. We learned to take care of one another and, as we got older, to look out for the younger campers. After all, those first-year campers who slept in the main house had to fall asleep with Bristletop's eyes right below them. It was a rite of passage we all had been through, just like our initiations on the mountaintop on our first Friday as campers.

On Sunday mornings, on the banks of Bear Creek, Mrs. Kidd led all ninety-six of us seven- to fourteen-year-olds in hymns. Those songs, coupled with the ones around the campfires and the beauty of the landscape that was so different from Grand Prairie, turned me into a little hill country Transcendentalist with a flattop. "Rock of Ages," "Amazing Grace," and "Bringing in the Sheaves" were no more the stuff of the summer musicals than were "This Land Is Your Land"

and "Blowin' in the Wind." They were about something much larger than a flower girl and a professor or a surrey with a fringe on top or Fernando's hideaway. They spoke to being part of something bigger than a romantic couple or a family singing act that featured kids in clothes made from curtains. When the shadows were dancing on the creek's banks and a light breeze was blowing, I was moved to tears as we sang. I felt that I had been there before. It was strange and wonderful—and difficult to describe. I tried to write about it in my letters home. Fath responded that he totally understood my "getting misty." We never really talked about why I got misty or whether other campers did, because talking about it would somehow take away its magic.

On closing day in 1962, when I was eleven and Fath was forty-six, I took him to Bear Creek while Steve was showing Mother around. I tried to describe what I had felt there, but could only say, "This is my favorite place. I wish you could have been here on one of those mornings."

He looked at me, a little aspiring Ralph Waldo Emerson in a cowboy shirt and a straw hat, and grinned. Then he said, "Dave, thanks for sharing this. It means more to me than you know." Then he, who was one of the world's great huggers, hugged me longer and harder than usual. He smelled like Chesterfields and the river and was, I knew, very happy in that moment. So was I.

I also vividly remember an afternoon with Fath the following summer. It was the day of the March on Washington. School had not started back up, and Fath had closed his office early, which he rarely did, in order to watch Martin Luther King Jr.'s speech at home with us. We were all there in front of our television— Fath, Mother, Steve, our sister, Melissa, and a few people from Fath's office, his receptionist, Virginia, and Uncle Lionel, the dentist with the slow drill. "Look at all those people!" he kept saying, tears on his cheeks and as misty as I had ever seen him. "This is a day we'll remember forever," he told us, barely able to get the words out. He added, "There are even some movie stars and singers there. Good for them."

A few years later, about the time I started hearing about Dylan because some friends had told me about him, I began lobbying for Top 40 on the car radio. Part of my case rested upon the point that Dylan had sung at the March on Washington and in Mississippi with Pete Seeger the month before. "I heard that too," Fath said as he lit a cigarette. "He did a good thing, but he's not Sinatra. Listen to 'Fly Me to the Moon,' Dave. Now there's a song. It's almost as good as 'Smile.'" It was one of the few times I thought Fath a typical dad. But I forgave him because, even though I knew better than to share such information with my friends, I did think "Fly Me to the Moon" was alright, for what it was. I liked "Smile" even better, which was a very un-teenage kind of thought and certainly should remain unspoken.

Those friends who gave me the ammunition to argue for Top 40 were Steve Hodges and Jimmy Chastain. A year ahead of me in school and members of the Latin Club, they were to Grand Prairie High School what the Great Books group was to the town. That is, they were few and viewed as kind of quirky. Hodges was heavyset with a thick head of hair and wore glasses. He smelled like he smoked cigarettes. He always had an irreverent quip about whatever topic was before us. Chastain was tall, thin, and clean-cut. He was a minister's son with excellent manners. His shirttails were almost always out and, apparently, he had a small rebellious streak or he would not have been hanging out with Hodges.

We got to know each other in Mrs. Powell's Latin classes, which were, along with Mr. Knox's theater ones, where the quirky kids converged. The suspended athletes and pretty girls gravitated to Mr. Knox. The academic achievers went toward Mrs. Powell. She was a red-haired woman who had gone to Rice, spoke several languages, flew small airplanes, and loved going fishing with her husband, Bill. She didn't seem to think that we were all that different from the athletes, the agricultural and shop students, or the marching band kids. She pushed us to study, but also laughed with us about things around town, like how the Baptist church would always schedule a social the night of the school dance. She shared our dislike of the cafeteria food and the lack of time that we had to eat it. We discussed television and movies and music, as well as Latin, in her class. We had even seen her and Bill in town on weekends, faces flush and laughing hard with Mrs. Hurley, the history teacher we all called by her first name, which was Zoe. Mr. Knox and Mrs. Carletti, the geometry teacher, also spent time with them. We liked them because, unlike most of our teachers, they never talked down to us. Nor did they let us slide when we were out of line, which we grudgingly respected because they were so funny and smart. Mr. Williams, the school principal, never granted our request that one of them replace Mr. Flewharty, the senior math teacher, as student council advisor. We had our suspicions about why this was the case.

For a good part of my junior year, Hodges and Chastain were bohemian big brothers to me. They talked about getting out of Grand Prairie and going two hundred miles south to Austin. "In Austin, beautiful girls go for guys like us," they told me one memorable night. It was nice to hear that there was a promised land three hours away, even though I wasn't quite sure how "guys like us" translated. One night we drove thirty minutes to Oak Lawn Avenue in Dallas and saw *What's New Pussycat?* We had heard that it was "scandalous" and seen some pictures in *Playboy*. All those beautiful women up on screen dancing with Peter O'Toole made me wonder if that was what was going on in Austin and other faraway places. Another time, Hodges and Chastain urged me to go to Wray's, the record store on Main Street, to ask for the headphones and to listen to *Blonde on Blonde*. "Look at the album cover. That's what girls in Austin like," Hodges told me with great authority and absolutely no supporting evidence.

They also kept talking about a club in Fort Worth called The Cellar. We finally went there before they graduated. Waitresses, some of them in bikinis or at least bikini tops, served setups. There were cushions on the floor in front of the stage. There were also bouncers, the first I had ever seen. With my razor-cut hair and polished shoes, I was totally out of place. It wasn't at all like *What's New Pussycat?* or *Rowan and Martin's Laugh-In*, a new television show with a cute girl named Goldie Hawn, who breathlessly said "Sock it to me!" in a way that very much appealed to the quirky ones among us. To my great disappointment, The Cellar reminded me more of the bus station than of Paris in the movies or of Los Angeles on television. Hodges and Chastain seemed to thoroughly enjoy the place. I faked my way through it all and was glad to get home to my bed, where I could listen to the White Sox game on my transistor radio and hope for another Flynn movie soon.

Although I had heard a few Dylan songs, ones that played on the radio and the ones that Hodges and Chastain talked about constantly, I preferred the Four Tops, The Temptations, Stevie Wonder, and all those dance tunes, even though I was only a dancer in my head. I also felt more comfortable with the music of Peter, Paul, and Mary or Simon and Garfunkel than with that of Dylan. "Leaving on a Jet Plane" went down much easier for me than did "Subterranean Homesick Blues" or "Like a Rolling Stone." At that point in my life, Dylan just sang too fast or too slow and sounded angrier than I wanted to be. I tried to get it, but just did not.

I was more taken with "Leaving on a Jet Plane," a song written by John Denver and performed by Peter, Paul, and Mary, because it fed right into another imagined world I was building around airports. In this one people were flying away to great adventures in Europe or South America or returning home to adoring families who had missed them terribly while they were away at college. Dallas Love Field became my favorite place to go on my incredibly disappointing dates. We would drive to the airport, buy a couple of Dr. Peppers, and watch people come and go. I would start a story, usually a variation on a Simon and Garfunkel song, hoping that my date would jump in and play along. Either my stories about hitchhiking from Saginaw and riding the bus with a man whose bowtie was really a camera were not the gems I thought they were or the partners I picked weren't the storytelling types. Probably both were true—and much more—on those nights. I listened to Van Morrison's "Brown Eyed Girl" and kept wondering where mine was. Discouraged but not defeated, I figured that perhaps a guy like me would have better luck with storytelling and dating when I went to college. Maybe Hodges and Chastain were right about that even though they had been way off about The Cellar.

Two television programs that I watched a few years earlier also spoke to me about the kind of people I would meet in my life after Grand Prairie. The first was *Hootenanny*, a show that traveled to and broadcast from college campuses in 1963 and 1964. The songs the students sang reminded me of the ones I had heard around the fire at Friday Mountain. I learned that Bob Dylan had written some of them, like "Blowin' in the Wind" and "The Times They Are a Changin'," both of which I liked very much because they were about social justice, even if the second one still sounded a bit angrier than I wanted it to. University life, at least through the lens of *Hootenanny*, looked like a coeducational summer camp of social activists or a Latin Club convention where people were actually having fun. I couldn't wait to get there.

My other favorite program, *That Was The Week That Was*, satirized political events and had a great blonde singer named Nancy Ames, who belted out its theme song. She wore a short black dress and displaced Olivia de Havilland in my affections. No one I went to school with reminded me of her. "TW3," as Fath and I called it, took on some of those Rathbones in American politics. Right there on the same screen where I had seen Errol Flynn, I was getting a light dose of civics from people who clearly were not happy with American political life and were willing to make jokes about the bomb and Lyndon Johnson and race. When both programs were taken off the air, I took it personally. Fath did as well, but told me, "Don't worry, Dave. History is on our side."

I nodded as I wondered what he meant. He would roll out "history is on our side" whenever one of our candidates or teams came in second, as they did more often than not. Like Dr. King, he believed that the long arc of history bent toward justice. I heard "history is on our side" almost as much as "he's more to be pitied than censured."

The only thing he said more frequently was "keep the faith." He used it for everything from my response to the Yankees losing the 1960 World Series when Bill Mazeroski hit that home run to my doubts, a few years later, that any girl would ever like my stories. Fath told me to keep the faith. All I saw at the time was that the World Series came around but once a year, and the kinds of girls I was most drawn to were most drawn to guys in blue jean jackets and frequent trouble. My observation about pretty girls became part of a large file of perplexing mysteries I was keeping under the title of "Punky's Dilemma," in tribute to one of my favorite Simon and Garfunkel songs. In my secret life, I was Punky trying to become Errol Flynn by way of Ralph Waldo Emerson, a transformation that even I knew would take some serious doing.

In my last year of high school, when Hodges and Chastain had moved on to Austin and while I worked after school at One Hour Martinizing, the local dry cleaners, I began my reinvention project in earnest. When my maternal grandmother, Helen Opalski, had asked me what I wanted for graduation, I—or, more accurately, some spirit that came along once in a blue moon and put words in my mouth—blurted out "a blue jean jacket." Mother disapproved. Fath said nothing, but smiled in what I took to be amused support. When my jacket arrived from the store in Wilkes Barre, Pennsylvania, I started working on making it look like the jackets of the outlaws with the beautiful girls. In those pre-stonewash days, I repeatedly drove my 1967 GTO over it in the cleaners' parking lot. My two best friends, Morrie Pickler and Mike Mooneyham, worked with me at the cleaners and were clearly entertained by my project.

Moon and I had spent a lot of time driving around listening to Simon and Garfunkel's *Bookends* and had recently become fond of *The Freewheelin' Bob Dylan*, an older album but one that felt less "radical" to us than all that electric music on *Highway 61 Revisited*. We had started learning some of Dylan's story. Therefore, Moon sort of understood what I was going for with the jacket.

"He left Minnesota," I told Moon without having to say Dylan's name, "and just went up to New York and met Woody Guthrie and started singing in coffeehouses. Look at him on that street in New York with that girl. He's not wearing slacks and a sports coat." Morrie, who knew me even better than Moon did and preferred Roger Miller to Simon and Garfunkel or Dylan, just shook his head, as many of my loved ones would do at various developmental flashpoints in my life. I attributed it to Morrie's growing up in Tennessee, a place that I imagined was even less sympathetic than Texas to "Hootenanny types," as he called the new tribe I told him I wanted to join.

Undeterred by the lack of enthusiastic support from my friends for either my jacket project or the much larger thing it represented, I convinced the Martinizing seamstress Ada to sew a large patch from corporate headquarters across the back of my nicely fading jacket. The patch was rectangular, about six by ten inches, white with green trim, and had a red rose cutting across our motto, "Fresh as a Flower in Just One Hour," at a forty-five-degree angle. The motto was written in green stitching. I had convinced Morrie's dad, who owned the cleaners, to give the patch to me. It really tied the jacket together, as it were, and made it different from everyone else's. I was working on being a good bad boy with a sense of humor, a funny outlaw wearing my own denim poem. It was the first thing I had made with my hands since the driftwood lamps and multicolored lanyards at Friday Mountain, and I was pretty proud of it.

Getting my jacket ready was the high point of a tough summer. Although I liked the cultural truism that the summer after one graduates from high school is a major turning point in life, I did not much like the way mine was turning. Both my political heroes, Martin Luther King Jr. and Bobby Kennedy, had been killed. A month after Kennedy died, Fath did as well. I spent a lot of time with Morrie and Moon and a little bit of time with the girl I was dating. She was not a Love Field kind of a girl. But then again, in all fairness, I wasn't a barrel of laughs or good stories either. I wore out *Bookends* and thought its *"Kathy I'm lost," though I knew she was sleeping / "I'm empty and aching and I don't know why"* said it all. That summer some of Dylan's songs, ones like "When the Ship Comes In" and "Boots of Spanish Leather," started making sense to me. "When the Ship Comes In" gave me something to hang on to in the face of one political trauma after another. "Boots of Spanish Leather" perfectly captured what I felt when my first real girlfriend had broken up with me for a guy in a blue jean jacket. I was seventeen and at sea. I had my blue jean jacket and wanted to feel a change coming on, even though I had no clue what that might be or even what it might look like.

Like Benjamin in *The Graduate*, the big movie of the year, all I knew was that I wanted my future to be, as he told his father after thinking for a few seconds, "different." When Moon and I went with our dates to see Dustin Hoffman play the confused college graduate who is so inept in his first hotel rendezvous with Mrs. Robinson, we laughed at him. I did so much more to suggest my worldliness, which I was totally faking, than in response to Hoffman's amazing performance. The Simon and Garfunkel soundtrack hinted at something going on beneath the surface, something intimated by the shot of Benjamin on that airport moving walkway as "The Sounds of Silence" played and by "Scarborough Fair" accompanying Elaine's return to Berkeley.

I see all of that now, but in the summer of 1968 I was no more ready to get my mind around Benjamin's dilemma than I was to understand the Dylan lyrics I was beginning to spend time with. I had a few of the tools I needed. However, the truth was, and in the perfect words of the narrator with no name that I would soon meet in one of my English classes, "First I had to attend college."[4]

I went west to Stanford in 1968 without much more forethought than had gone into my asking Grandma for my blue jean jacket. I liked the idea of California, applied, got in, thanks to my essay about Mrs. Carletti's geometry class and, more likely, a letter of recommendation from Fath's buddy, New York City Mayor John V. Lindsay. A few weeks before I left Grand Prairie for California, I had watched the Democratic National Convention in Chicago, where people only a few years older than I were beaten up in the streets as they chanted words from "When the Ship Comes In." I noticed that the commentators gave Dylan credit for the words *the whole wide world is watching*, and I made some kind of loose connection with the March on Washington and how much had changed since then. I flew out of Love Field to San Francisco with my jacket, a typewriter, two suitcases, and many longings.

During my first month in Palo Alto I heard David Harris, the former student body president who had married Joan Baez, talk about resisting the war and going to prison to make a statement. I saw and heard Eldridge Cleaver, who was prohibited from speaking on University of California campuses, come to Stanford to roll out such Black Power concepts as "pussy power." Conscientious new student that I was, I wrote down the phrase, along with his words "the woman's place in the movement is on her back," in case we were someday tested by someone on what he said or how it related to the assigned reading in *Soul on Ice*. It also allowed me to avert my eyes from anyone who might see the embarrassment and bewilderment therein. B. Davie Napier, the chaplain who invited Cleaver to campus, gave a homily about placing the needle down on the wrong track of *Bookends* and hearing "Overs" as a song that he thought was

"America." It felt like a sermon tailor-made for me and the perfect conclusion to my totally disorienting freshman orientation. Dorothy's distance from Kansas in *The Wizard of Oz* was no greater than mine from Grand Prairie in the fall of 1968.

To complicate matters a bit more, I had been an A student all my life and made an F on my first paper. The assignment was to write an extended definition of any word, term, or phrase. I chose to write about "integrity" for Mr. Weston, a graduate student who had attended Sewanee and been an editor at something called *The Sewanee Review*. Initially I was delighted to discover that he had reproduced my paper anonymously for the class to read and discuss. I felt so confident seeing my work on that mimeographed sheet that, before we began discussing it, I calmly let it be known, particularly to Christine Russell, who was beautiful and sitting beside me, that I had written it, "just in case you need any help on your writing."

Shortly after the thorough routing of "Integrity," first by my classmates and then more diplomatically by Mr. Weston, I went back to Madera 208, my freshman dorm room, and told my roommate, Phil Brosterhous, that I was leaving school. Phil had played football at Servite a few years behind John Huarte, a recent Heisman Trophy winner who had played quarterback for Notre Dame. He also knew a lot about the Hittites, liked "Nights in White Satin" by a band called the Moody Blues, and thought that the film version of *A Man for All Seasons* worked perfectly if you just closed your eyes and listened to the language. On top of all that, he was also probably the nicest person I had ever met. In short, rooming with him and writing a paper like "Integrity" added up to my being even more out of my intellectual element at Stanford than I had been out of my social one back in Grand Prairie.

"What will you do?" Phil calmly asked.

"Well, I can't go home," I admitted. "It would just be too sad. Too much of a failure for me to admit." I thought for a while. Time slowed down. In that moment I really understood Dylan's words about having *no direction home*. I had been hearing those words for three years and finally knew what he meant. It was a very minor consolation. I blurted out, "I'm going to look into joining the circus. Trapeze women and all, you know."

Phil didn't bat an eye or shake his head. Instead, he said, "Sounds interesting, but you can't drop out until Monday. Let's go to San Francisco tonight and hear whoever is playing at Winterland."

It was all new to me. I had never heard of Winterland. All I knew was that there was no need to read R. R. Palmer's *History of the Modern World* or ten chapters of *Moby-Dick* for the following week's classes that I would not be around to attend. So, I put on my jacket, my Virginia Beach East Coast Surfing Championship T-shirt, and the closest thing I had to jeans, which was some light-brown corduroys. We went up 101, the same highway that Dustin Hoffman's Benjamin drove, to the city.

Winterland was a far cry from the Dallas Summer Musicals and The Cellar. I had never seen anything like it. It looked and sounded even better than *What's New Pussycat?* or *Laugh-In.* Tanned people with long hair were wearing clothes right out of those Errol Flynn movies. No one had to have a partner to dance or seemed to care how anyone danced, and people shared whatever they were drinking or smoking. The music was terrific, both dreamy and impossible not to dance to. The lyrics were about white birds and a girl named Sugar Magnolia. I thought about Hodges and Chastain, Morrie and Moon, my Love Field dates, Fath and Bobby Kennedy. I missed them all, but in good ways. I wasn't sad. I just wished they could see this and feel what I was feeling. The only thing that I had ever felt that compared to it was being by Bear Creek at Friday Mountain. This was much better, though, because it was coeducational and unsupervised.

On our way out, a girl with long red hair and terrific freckles came up to me and said, "Great jacket!" I looked at her and offered my summer creation to her. When she said, "That would be amazing!" I handed it to her, like some Lower Pacific Heights Sir Walter Raleigh covering a mud puddle or like Robin taking the reins of Maid Marian's horse as he walked her back to the road in Sherwood Forest. She did a double-take and then quickly kissed me on the cheek. It was the kiss of a new friend, one-half of the way friends greeted one another in French movies. The words "Fresh as a Flower in Just One Hour" shrank a bit more with each step she took, like the *Albatross* leaving port in *The Sea Hawk* or another disappearing West Texas town below the plane window when I had flown west a few weeks and another lifetime ago. I felt that history was on my side. I liked what it felt like to be in a new place with everything ahead of me. I was happier, and colder, than I had been in a long time.

Rather than joining the circus and pursuing trapeze women, I went to see Mr. Weston the following Monday. He was a very serious character, with wire-rimmed glasses, a narrow tie, and a stack of papers on his desk.

Bypassing all small talk, he asked me, "Mr. Gaines, what were you trying to say in your paper? Tell me in your own words, as simply as possible."

I told him that my major heroes—King, Kennedy, and my father—had all died that summer and that I was trying to figure out how to write about it. He asked me why I had not written those exact words rather than a string of abstractions with a sprinkling of inappropriate thesaurus choices like *grapples* as a noun and *nebulous* as an all-purpose adjective.

He then told me, "Specific examples are always preferable to abstractions, Mr. Gaines. You need first to figure out what you want to say and then to say it without trying to impress anyone." It was the first time anyone had told me this, although it would not be the last. He did not tell me I was capable of doing the work or encourage me in the slightest. He let it be known, by looking at his watch and stack of papers, that our visit was finished. As he was walking me out, he offered to work with me on future drafts. I felt like I had been given a second chance. I awkwardly thanked him for his time.

Walking back to his desk, he added, "I'm sorry for your losses, Mr. Gaines. Continue to look for new heroes. They are out there."

I did go back to Mr. Weston's office a few times and got some suggestions on my drafts. Besides writing an extended definition, I also wrote critical summaries, process papers, imitations of other writers (because I liked something we read about a "transparent eyeball," I chose Emerson), and bibliographic entries. No more of my papers were reproduced. I wrote shorter, clearer sentences and made Bs. Then, one week near the end of the quarter, a comic sketch that I wrote about a Saturday night in Madera caused Mr. Weston to write the following brief comment after my final paragraph: "This is vivid and very funny, Mr. Gaines. You should read James Joyce's 'Nighttown' episode. Very good. A-" I wanted to frame that page and put it on my wall. Instead, I memorized his sixteen words and my grade. I tried to read Joyce.

A few quarters later, I declared my major in English and began hanging out with other English majors, all of whom listened to a lot of music and, it seemed, liked quoting Dylan more than anyone else. They were particularly fond of the lines *Ezra Pound and T. S. Eliot / Fighting in the Captain's tower* and *You've been through all of F. Scott Fitzgerald's books / You're very well read / It's well known.* "He would have been an English major if he had stayed in school," my fellow major Bob Rigdon told me. A few years later, Rigdon began one of his personal statements for law school with *I started out on burgundy / But soon hit the harder stuff.* Even though he did not get into that law school, we voted that application our personal favorite and Rigdon a brave guy to try such a stunt.

Dylan also started turning up on more of the turntables I was hearing at parties as well as on Stanford's student radio station, which was my introduction to radio that was neither easy listening nor Top 40. Now and then one of my contemporaries, usually from California or New England, would devote an entire program to Dylan's music. They even had titles for their themed programs, like "Subterranean Homesick Blues" and "Rainy Day Women." Those programs were terrific research projects built around great songs. I was stunned by how much Dylan had written, how much it varied, and how he could write and sing about all the things my new friends and I were interested in—politics, romance, sex, drugs—in language that we had to work at to understand, just like the novels and poems and movies we were discussing in and out of our classes. No one I had heard or read came close to him in terms of so much food for thought and conversation with the kinds of people I enjoyed being around.

Dylan even made his way into some of my classes, like twentieth-century American literature in which Bill Chace showed Erich von Stroheim's *Greed* one evening and used part of *Nashville Skyline* for the soundtrack. A 1924 movie that looked a bit like *The Gold Rush* but had a totally un-Chaplin view of how things turned out, it was greatly enhanced by hearing Dylan and Johnny Cash singing "Girl from the North Country" as ZaSu Pitts made her way around San Francisco. We started referring to Chace, who was a Pound and Eliot scholar but clearly liked Dylan and worked him into his lectures on Allen Ginsberg as "Wild Bill." Walter Sokel's lectures on world literature were such performances that I frequently convinced a friend to go with me to hear about Kafka or Joyce or Proust.

One day, when Sokel asked if any contemporary writers were comparable to Dickens, I had the audacity to raise my hand and say, "Bob Dylan might be." A few of my fellow English majors in the class—Rigdon among them—seemed to like the suggestion.

Sokel, who had written about German Expressionism as well as Kafka, thought for almost a full minute before saying, "That's a very interesting answer. It's not the first time I have heard that. Perhaps I should listen to him." A couple of girls nodded at me as we walked out of class.

I started hanging out at Kepler's Books in Menlo Park and making pilgrimages to City Lights in North Beach, where photographs of Dylan decorated the stairwell up to the poetry room. I began buying records, even though I didn't yet have a turntable, and growing my hair because everyone else was. *Bringing*

It All Back Home replaced *Bookends* on the top of my short stack. I became obsessed with "Mr. Tambourine Man" and played it whenever I could sneak in some turntable time. *Far from the twisted reach of crazy sorrow* sounded to me like the perfect place to be and perhaps where I was headed.

These changes did not play well when I went home for Christmas. Morrie and Moon, who were attending Howard Payne University, a Baptist school in Brownwood, Texas, asked me what was going on. Something in their voices made me suspect that they thought I had been captured by aliens. My long-distance romance with the girl I had dated during the last few months of my senior year ended with a whimper. It was her idea, but I knew it was a good one. Steve, who had grown four inches in as many months, told me how rough things had been for him at home without me and that he was already planning his escape to Austin. My mother let me know that three of the many things she was not happy about were my changing my major from political science to English, my wearing jeans instead of slacks, and, as she put it with that emphasis none of us ever wanted to hear, "your hair." Right before I boarded my plane, Moon gave me a cassette that included his rendition of "Just Like Tom Thumb's Blues," one of my favorite Dylan songs at the time. Moon was a good guitar player and his version of Dylan's song began, "When you're lost in the rain in Palo Alto / and it's Easter time too." It was fun and promising to switch *Palo Alto* for *Juarez*, and I knew it was a gift. But it took a turn for me when I heard, "And picking up Dave who just arrived here from the coast / Who looked so fine at first / But left looking just like a ghost." Maybe I, rather than the song, took the turn. Whatever the case, I chose not to hear the rest of it because it felt like just one more judgment from a world that I was leaving behind. I told myself it was part of the soundtrack to a movie filled with rearview mirror shots.

My new friends understood all of it—me, my hair, Dylan, Winterland, City Lights—a lot better than did my old friends. For example, in September 1969 I met Bob Payne who, like Rigdon, Brosterhous, several other sophomores, and me, had moved into the Alpha Sig house. Unlike me, Bob had wallpapered his room with wrappers from the barbecue place where he worked. The labor that he put into the undertaking was akin to what the pointillist painters I had read about did. I liked the whimsical weirdness of walls covered in Arby's wrappers. It seemed to come from the same kind of worldview that would put a Martinizing patch on the back of a blue jean jacket and run over it repeatedly in a GTO. On top of that, the very first words Bob said to me, without ever taking off his headphones, were, "I've got Bob Dylan going all through me." He was listening to *John Wesley Harding* and studying for his German class and made his announcement perfectly deadpan. If I had read *Catch-22* at that point in my life, its first line—"It was love at first sight"—would have come to mind.[5]

Another friend, Mike Pinkerton, was an English major and a Colorado native who was addicted to *Nashville Skyline*'s "Country Pie." I was not as fond of it as he was, but it was worth getting through to hear "Tonight I'll Be Staying Here with You," which came up next. "Bridge Over Troubled Water," which seemed somehow connected to Dylan's songs, was always playing in Bob Polk's room. I often dropped in and stayed for "So Long, Frank Lloyd Wright." Crosby, Stills, and Nash had their champions, as did Buffalo Springfield.

Of course, not everyone fancied Dylan or Americana. But almost everyone took their music seriously. When Ed Oster was on deadline for a debate tournament, he played *Creedence Clearwater Revival*, and particularly "Born on the Bayou," into the early hours of the morning. His typewriter, on which he was pounding out note cards, turned into one more instrument behind John Fogerty's vocals. About the time Oster would go to bed, pre-med Eric Batchelor would wake up and crank up the Rolling Stones's *Let It Bleed* for sunrise. John Brunsman, one of the few of us with any kind of a singing voice, leaned to Laura Nyro or Sly and the Family Stone when he wasn't bemoaning his hometown Cubs' latest collapse. Rick Samco and I roomed together for a quarter and spent a good bit of time listening to Jefferson Airplane's *Volunteers* and the Beatles' *Abbey Road* on his amazing sound system.

Whenever one Catherine "Cricket" Bird, an English major I briefly dated, would call on the fraternity house phone, someone would find a way to get Lennon and McCartney's "Drive My Car" on a speaker and turn it up as high as possible. It was both a nod to my generosity with my vehicle and a form of speculation about the nature of Cricket's interest in me.

My year of living in the fraternity house was like inhabiting a hall of speakers as distinguished from a house of mirrors. The only thing the experience resembled more than turning the radio dial and getting one great song after another was turning half a dozen radio dials to different stations all at once and getting six different great songs. Dylan came up as frequently as anyone on those dials. In fact, sometimes two or three Dylans would come up all at once because even then, as I was beginning to hear on the student station and in the hallways, there were already multiple Dylans. One day, within the course of forty steps, I heard pieces of Dylan singing "Lay Lady Lay," "Visions of Johanna," and "Oxford Town." It was a jigsaw puzzle for my ears. I had read about the cubism of "Nude Descending a Staircase" and the "cut-up method" of *Naked Lunch*. In a way, we were living both techniques—and then some—each time we walked through the hallways of the Alpha Sig house. I loved it.

I gravitated toward the house's singer-songwriter camp rather than its psychedelic jam band one. One night, while I was sleeping, a major Cream fan—I suspected Jim Prickett, although it was never confirmed—painted yellow submarines on my glasses as a commentary on my preference for the Beatles over the Stones. It all reminded me of Fath's description of the divisions on his destroyer, the USS *Swanson*, during World War II. Whereas he and his shipmates had, as he put it, "refought the Civil War," my housemates and I divided along musical lines. We believed that what we listened to was a major part of who we were, and it was hardly coincidental that I did the majority of my undergraduate partying with Bob Payne, Bob Rigdon, and Mike Pinkerton, word people who pretty much stayed on burgundy.

That first summer, rather than go back to Grand Prairie, I worked for New York City's Housing Department with Ed Oster and our mutual friend Fred Mann, who also preferred the Beatles to the Stones. He contributed the White Album to our collection of three cassettes, which we played almost every night on my Sony tape recorder. Ed brought Big Brother and the Holding Company's *Cheap Thrills* rather than Creedence, which he only had on vinyl. I pitched in with *Blonde on Blonde* because, I reasoned that, like the White Album, it was a double album. We had our own little concert almost every night in our fifth-floor walkup at 514 Madison Avenue. We got to know those albums the way normal nineteen-year-olds without much in their heads would, which was obsessively. We weren't very keen on "Revolution #9," but thought "Back in the U.S.S.R." and "The Continuing Saga of Bungalow Bill" were great because they were both funny and had some serious guitar work. George's guitar on "While My Guitar Gently Weeps" was even better. Whenever one of our friends or siblings had a birthday, we would call them up long distance on our apartment phone, which had mistakenly not been disconnected, and play "Birthday" as high as the Sony would crank, which was nowhere near loud enough. We reveled in what we agreed was Janis Joplin's orgasm on "Piece of My Heart."

But most of all, we played "Visions of Johanna" and "Desolation Row," digging deeper and deeper into Dylan's lyrics, quoting them to one another, and deciding that we were just three more characters living on Desolation Row. We joked about sniffing drainpipes and reciting the alphabet. The album provided us with a lingua franca as we rode the subway or wandered around the Village. New York was Broadway Joe Namath's town that summer, but we had our eyes peeled for Dylan. We never saw him, although we had heard he was living in either Woodstock or Greenwich Village and saw a few people who seemed to be trying to look like him as, truth be told, I was starting to try to do with my spotty beard and wire-rimmed glasses.

In the evenings I parked cars in a garage on Second Avenue and read Herman Hesse novels. The job was equal parts stress, boredom, and questionable transactions seemingly linked to insurance scams. The silver lining was a Jamaican named Billy whose voice was a dead ringer for Stevie Wonder's. When he came up the ramp from the basement, he would always be singing "My Cherie Amour." It was a beautiful thing.

One night I asked Billy if he knew any Dylan. He just laughed and said, "No, college boy. The man can't sing." I took no offense because I wasn't listening to Dylan primarily for his singing. I would defend his delivery back in the campus music wars, but just didn't know if the argument would fly in the garage. And I certainly didn't want to do anything to jeopardize my hearing Stevie's sweet and dreamy words bouncing off those concrete walls. For me, hearing Billy sing Stevie's words was right up there with the Mets' pennant run, the posters of Woodstock in the subways, and Neil Armstrong's televised step that summer.

The following spring I moved out of the fraternity house and started living on Kingsley Avenue with Marie, the brown-eyed girl I married a few years later. She liked my stories, went to Sokel's classes and *Citizen Kane* with me, came from a big, lively family, had a sly sense of humor, and was always in motion. I once told her, as a compliment, "Your family is like a Fellini movie," and she responded, with some edge in her voice, "Yeah. You're watching it and I'm living it." When we moved to Austin in January 1973, I spent $30 of our only $100 on records. It's an early music story that, for better or worse, set the tone for much of our marriage.

I had come back to our $80-a-month garage apartment beside a nine-hole municipal golf course with Traffic's *John Barleycorn Must Die*, the Who's *Who's Next*, Joni Mitchell's *Blue*, *Close to the Edge* by Yes, Bob's *Another Side of Bob Dylan*, and a backup copy of the eponymous *Crosby, Stills, and Nash*. Wide-eyed newlywed that I was, I announced, "Look what we just got!" as I pulled our five new—and one backup—albums out of a brown paper bag.

Observant character that she was, Marie pointed out, "We don't even have a stereo!" She wasn't laughing.

I put as much of my heart as possible into saying, "But someday we will, and we'll be glad we got these at such a good price." I kept the canceled check, #001, I had written but never talked about it again. It would have been kind of like Ilsa talking to Rick about Paris in *Casablanca*, "poor salesmanship," as he put it.

The fault lines in our marriage often surfaced around music. It was not so much that we disagreed about what we liked but rather that, as far as Marie was concerned, I spent too much time listening to, talking about, and being guided by music when I wasn't talking about and being guided by movies, writing, or baseball. For example, one night Led Zeppelin's "Stairway to Heaven" was playing on our totally excellent, brand-new turntable when I took some key words about life's journey to heart. The next day I told Marie that I had decided to withdraw from law school. This struck her as almost as crazy, although I think I remember her using the word "impulsive," as my buying the albums. I said that I could see how it might seem that way to her, but that to me it was hardly *impulsive* if everything for the past year had been leading to that moment. I left law school in good standing and with no intention of ever coming back. When Dean Keaton asked me why I was withdrawing, I told him, "Led Zeppelin." He responded that he had never heard that specific reason or anything remotely like it. He then asked me if I wanted it in my record and I told him that it was fine with me.

I was very fond of venues like Soap Creek Saloon and Armadillo World Headquarters and events like Blues Women Night at Antone's and Willie Nelson's Fourth of July picnics. Marie did not share these particular enthusiasms. This was in large part because she, who had a lot of Carlos Santana in her past and liked the blues women quite a bit, was one of the most politically committed and professionally ambitious people I have ever known. This led her to working sixty to seventy hours a week in the city Planning Department and frequently bemoaning the fact that "Texas has no real zoning." She was on track to run for city council. A few people much more in the know than I said she would be mayor someday.

I often got a sense of her day by listening to the zoning board and city council meetings on KUT, Austin's National Public Radio affiliate. I marveled at her answers to complicated land-use questions. Invariably, Marie's answers were direct, frontloaded with the yea or nay, and then followed by the numbered reasons for the recommendation. It was the exact opposite of the shaggy dog stories I told and liked listening to.

We agreed fully that Texans' views of so-called "highest and best use" usually translated into no awareness of the public good. I got too upset by some of the cases that we had discussed and that I then heard play out on KUT. It seemed that *power and greed and corruptible seed seem to be all that there is*, as Dylan put it in "Blind Willie McTell" right around that time. I began questioning how Marie kept her shoulder to that particular wheel while recognizing that I did not have the patience for the process. Many nights I cooked as I listened to music or watched baseball or read a Vintage Contemporary and tried to guess the time of Marie's return, based upon how the docket was running. Sometimes the meetings ended as early as nine. When the city started growing like gangbusters in the early Eighties, one in the morning was more the norm and three was not out of the question.

Beginning in 1981, KUT deejay Larry Monroe was charged with playing music when the council was in recess or closed session. He called the show "Phil Music," and the mayor even got in the habit of calling for "a Phil Music motion." Larry's repertoire was somewhere between 25 and 100 percent Dylan, depending upon his mood and the events around us. Through him, I learned about Townes Van Zandt and Butch Hancock and Lucinda Williams and a lot of old blues people. Every May, right around Dylan's birthday, "Phil Music" would have what Larry called "The Dylan Birthday Salute." He liked pointing out that the allusion came from "She Belongs to Me" and its line *salute her when her birthday comes*. He would start with Dylan's birth in Duluth, always naming the obstetrician who delivered him, and then let the previous year's Dylan developments, whether they were a new album or a particular tour, guide his commentary and selections. He had a great enthusiastic voice with a hint of his native Indiana in it, never went on too long, and knew more about Dylan than anyone I had ever heard. I rarely missed the program and started taping it to play the cassettes during the week. Following Monroe's trails ended up costing us some money for the supplementary materials I had to have. It also brought me a lot of collateral joy. One such joy was hearing an early release of "Things Have Changed" in 2000 and Larry's masterfully concise introduction: "Bob's gotten back his sense of humor." I liked hearing that because it got me thinking about what I had been missing in Dylan for a while as well as about a large part of his appeal for me.

Now and then on council nights Marie would also listen to Larry, just to clear the cobwebs. She liked "Slow Train" for its beat, questioned the sexual politics of "Sweetheart Like You," and was "appalled that anyone would say *you must forgive me my unworthiness.*" I offered something quite lame like "one bad line doesn't make a bad song" and marveled that she could hear such things in the middle of a worknight. We had some good disagreements over Dylan.

As it turned out, many of our best times involved music. Marie often scribbled Lucinda Williams or Bonnie Raitt lyrics on cards to me, and she was particularly fond of Lucinda's "Lines around Your Eyes" with its words about the singer's challenging partner. We saw Dylan's *Street Legal* show with our best friends Tom and Pat and played him on our sound system, which I had wired through the house and out onto the deck. We saw Bonnie Raitt two nights in a row with Donna Squyres and our attorney Jim Cousar, who had given me his vinyl copy of the very first Dylan album. Marie and I had a standing date at Hut's, a burger place where Angela Strehli played on Tuesdays from ten to one. Angela sang, Mark "Kaz" Kazanoff played sax, and some of our Planning Department and magazine writer friends would show up to drink and dance.

One particularly memorable night in the middle of a particularly high-volume, and even higher-intensity, month in the Planning Department, a night that I wasn't betting on her being there, Marie came strolling in around midnight in her cornflower-blue linen suit, ordered a shot of tequila, and danced with me until they shut the place down. We had met dancing to Creedence's "Fortunate Son" at a party in Palo Alto in 1970, and our first gifts to one another were Carole King's *Tapestry* (from me to Marie) and the lyrics of Buffalo Springfield's "I Am a Child" (from Marie to me). It was hardly surprising that through all our differences, we often ended up together at music.

Marie's final gift to me before she died was two tickets to see Dylan for my fortieth birthday. She had been incurably ill for a few years and not well enough to go to the show. I was torn about going to the show, but she encouraged me to take someone. Ambivalently, I went. I gave the extra ticket to the first person I saw. I heard Dylan play three songs, one of which was "Tangled Up in Blue." It was one of my favorite songs even though, or maybe because, its *We always did feel the same / We just saw it from a different point of view* struck me as pretty close to the story of our marriage. It was raining, I was worried, and I left early to go 780 feet above sea level to Mount Bonnell, a park on a hill in west Austin. I wanted to let things wash over and pour out of me. Dylan had just released "Shooting

Star" and it, even more than "Tangled Up in Blue," captured so much of what I felt about our life together in Marie's last years. I still feel a lot of the same things when I hear *seen a shooting star tonight / And I thought of you / You were trying to break into another world / A world I never knew.* It's a powerful, sad, beautiful song about different trajectories and things unsaid. Bob has always been good at that.

The next morning our four-year-old daughter, Rachel, asked me if I had seen Dylan. For some reason, she added, "Did he wear your raincoat, Dad?" Maybe she had heard Leonard Cohen's "Famous Blue Raincoat," the Jennifer Warnes version, one too many times. It, alternating with Bonnie and Lucinda and Nick Drake and Van Morrison and Joni and Dylan, was on our turntable a lot.

Rach had already been heavily indoctrinated in Dylan lore, given that I had been telling her bedtime stories under the working title of *The Keybelly Chronicles.* The stories revolved around her favorite toy, a small, soft white bear we called Baby Bear. Baby Bear had a key in his stomach that we turned to play something akin to "Twinkle, Twinkle, Little Star" on his internal jukebox. All of Baby Bear's adventures grew out of Dylan's biography as I had learned it from Larry Monroe and my reading. Rach heard about Baby Bear's name change from Little Zimmerman, his little brother Davey Bear, his motorcycle accident, a house called Big Pink where other bears named Robbie and Levon and Rick and Garth hung out with him, his kids who called him Pa, the cabin in Utah, and his band. We didn't talk about his divorce or his born-again phase. She was too young for that. I never ran out of chapters and liked the blend of adventure, romance, and caution built into these *Chronicles* (I also felt both vindicated and prescient when Dylan took part of the name for the title of his memoir).

When our son, Sid, was old enough, I started telling him these stories as well when I wasn't reading him *The Little Prince* or William Joyce's latest book, be it *Dinosaur Bob and His Adventures with the Family Lazardo* or *An Afternoon with Wilbur Robinson.* In the spirit of being intentional about helping our kids appreciate Dylan, one of the first things I made sure of was that both Rach and Sid knew how to say *the vandals took the handles.* After all, I reasoned, what is cuter than a little kid quoting "Subterranean Homesick Blues"? Whenever either of them would say it, Marie was sure to laugh. It was but one of the many things Rach and Sid did that made her smile. In those sweet moments I could see the lines around her eyes.

Opportunities to convey Dylan lessons and lore kept arising over my years of parenting. When I married Norma, a *Scorpio sphinx in a calico dress* who had two kids of her own, Christopher and Kelley joined Rach and Sid hearing about Dylan. Although his albums were never the consensus road-trip picks of our blended family—the Beatles and Sinatra were, an irony that would not have been lost upon Fath—Dylan's music and various stories about him kept popping up. The up-tempo, fiddle-rich version of "Forever Young" was frequently on when we were cooking dinner or out by the pool because it encapsulated all those wishes (*may God bless and keep you always*) so many parents have for their children. Nor was I above using cue cards, as Dylan did in the scene that opened *Dont Look Back*, for the milestone home videos like graduations or road trips. For those efforts, I worked hard on my printing, being deadpan, and not overusing the *WHAT?* card.

Christopher, who has grown up to play some killer guitar in three bands to this point in time, was particularly fond of singing *Oh, Mama, can this really be the end* whenever "Stuck Inside of Mobile with the Memphis Blues Again" came on. His best preadolescent cover, in a perfectly wry boy-man voice, came from the backseat one morning as we were driving out of Garner State Park. It was as good as hearing *the vandals took the handles* because, for me, there is nothing better than knowing that the torch is being passed. Sid and his buddies Sean Mooney, Patrick McCullough, and Renzie Chipman always requested "Hurricane" on their way to their fifth-grade soccer games, which made me very happy, even though it was far from my favorite Dylan song. Around that time, they also sat patiently through my detailed account of the motorcycle accident one evening over pizza and before watching BASE*ketball* on the VCR. One day when I picked up Sid from his fourth-grade classes, he got in the backseat and went right into his best eleven-years-old-going-on-seventy rendition of the Band's song about Nazareth, Crazy Chester, Miss Moses, and Fanny. It confirmed my suspicion that although he had had a bad day, he knew how to do it justice. Kelley selected Dylan as the subject of her Theology I project on "Prophets" at St. Michael's Catholic Academy. She kept her notes in a folder labeled *BOBBY*. It was a term of endearment that I would like to take a bit of credit for putting in the ether, although it is just as likely that Kell channeled it, as she does so many linguistic things. Without much guidance from me, she found the lyrics to "Long Gone," "Masters of War," "Blowin' in the Wind," and "The Times They Are A-Changin.'" Her paper of December 3, 1999, began with *But I ain't no prophet or a prophet's son* and then cited Amos 7:14 ("I was no prophet, neither was I a prophet's son") before concluding, "I think that prophets are everywhere and that listening to this kind of music can inspire others to stand up for what is right."[6] It was better than anything I ever wrote in high school—and possibly college, for that matter. Mr. Weston and Bill Stott would have approved. I was very proud.

Ten years after that, Rach graduated from the College of Santa Fe with a degree in contemporary music. One of her degree requirements was to organize a senior show consisting of both cover and original material. Norma and I had compared notes with her about the show as it was evolving, and we arranged to be there to see it with Christopher, Kelley, and Sid. Two of the kids' cousins, Jennifer and Adam, their uncle Bobby and his wife, Betsy, and their uncle David were also there representing the family. Dylan was not on the playlist, although Rach had sent me covers she did of "Tangled Up in Blue" and "Wagon Wheel." My hunch is that Rach knew that if she put any Dylan on the program I, who had grown exponentially more inclined to mistiness with parenthood, would not have had a snowball's chance in hell of hanging on. Even if she was not thinking this, she did the right thing. A few weeks before her graduation, she sent us the poster advertising the show. It was, in the style of Milton Glaser's iconic 1967 pop art poster of Dylan, a silhouette of her profile beneath her multicolored kaleidoscopic hair. On her shoulder in brown, in the same position that Glaser had DYLAN, was RACHEL. After a few days, when I had pulled enough of myself together, I had the image transferred to T-shirts for all of us so we could embarrass her yet one more time, as we did, at the show.

Norma was at the center of all of this—and more. She taught me how to be part of a family, and she kept us all together. She taught me a lot about music and art—and more about love and faith. Of course, there is a Dylan lyric that I thought about when Norma appeared in my life: *Something there is about you that moves with style and grace / I was in a whirlwind, now I'm in some better place.* Over our twenty years and counting together, we have had our adventures at home and on the road with the kids: at the beach and Disneyland, camping in Yellowstone, on road trips to Colorado, New Mexico, Arizona, Nevada, and Montana. One Christmas we went to New York, waited for our luggage beside Tony Bennett at La Guardia, and heard a busker sing "Deep in the Heart of Texas" to Rach on her sixteenth birthday while we stood in line for the ferry to the Statue of Liberty and Ellis Island. By then, the kids were old enough for the windshield tour of Greenwich Village and Dylan's old haunts, which I chalked up as essential cultural enrichment. Over our years together, we had numerous family meetings, swung at several piñatas, and spent hundreds of hours in and around our swimming pool. Literally and metaphorically, we have *been to the east and ... been to the west / And ... been out where the black winds roar.*

There have been some *black winds*, and I have not always been—and still am not—the husband or parent or friend I hoped to be. That is to say: my story should not be mistaken for one of those holiday letters about all my family's successes. Those letters, with far too much public happiness and self-congratulation for my taste, have always felt a bit creepy to me. They fly in the face of another Fath-ism: "The poker player with the winning hand never talks about having the cards." Trying to sneak in an un-ironic "it's all good" vibe would not be true to all that I have lived and much of what I have learned from listening to Dylan.

Instead, I like to think about what Dylan told interviewer Mikal Gilmore around the time he turned fifty and Gilmore asked him if he was happy. Dylan replied, "You know, these are yuppie words, happiness and unhappiness. It's not happiness or unhappiness, it's either blessed or unblessed." When Gilmore then asked Dylan if he felt blessed, he said, "Oh yeah. . . . Yeah, I do."[7] That's kind of the way I'm seeing it these days as well.

When I try to write about it all—about Norma, the kids, my in-laws, my brothers and sisters, my friends and teachers and students—I feel like I am getting ever closer to an answer to E. B. White's question, the one Fath told me was the key to it all. In that vein, when I first heard Dylan's "Sign on the Window" on *New Morning*, its final stanza caught my ear. Anyone who would end by singing *that must be what it's all about*, and twice at that, was playing with the idea of what his narrator wanted and the likelihood that some of his listeners might also be looking for the key to it all. The Dylan narrator in "Sign on the Window," whom I never mistook for Dylan because I have been well taught by my professors and by Dylan himself, said what he thought it was all about: *Build me a cabin in Utah / Marry me a wife, catch rainbow trout / Have a bunch of kids who call me "Pa."* I liked the sound of it a lot, even though I had not grown up seeing anything close to that, had not yet met either Marie or Norma, had not had a bunch of kids or been to Utah. I did what I had done so many times before, and would do so many times again, with so much of what Dylan sang and wrote: I stored it away somewhere in my memory, waiting until I was ready for it.

Dylan wrote about the cabin, the wife, and the kids as one version of *what it's all about.* He also wrote, over the years, about *the Grand Canyon at sunset,* words *pourin' off of every page / like it was written in my soul from me to you,* and countless other moments of clarity. We all have our own cabins and Grand Canyons and poems, and it is good that Dylan reminds us of the fact. In my life, there have been perfect meals and great songs and beautiful paintings and amazing movies and golf course epiphanies and classroom revelations and magical swims in rivers and oceans and, as the poet Robert Hass so perfectly put it, "moments when the body is as numinous / as words, days that are the good flesh continuing."[8] Most of the time, I have been blessed to share those experiences with the people I love; in fact, for me, such moments hardly seem possible without my loved ones. Like I admitted earlier, I am much more of an emotional and sentimental boy than a hip one, more of a family guy than a loner.

One more such moment came my way on November 1, 2012. It was Norma's birthday, and we stood twenty feet from Dylan as he played in Grand Prairie. We had seen him four times—for our first anniversary on the spur of the moment with scalped tickets at the Austin Music Hall, then on tour with Paul Simon in the Erwin Center, a few years later in San Antonio with Merle Haggard, and most recently at a minor league ballpark, where he headed a bill that included John Mellencamp and Willie Nelson. That night in Grand Prairie we were only five miles from the old location of Wray's Record Shop, where Hodges and Chastain had urged me to go hear *Blonde on Blonde* forty-six years earlier. We had come back to where it all began.

Bob was sitting sideways at his piano and playing "Things Have Changed." He had already sung *lot of water under the bridge, lot of other stuff too*, and it flew through my mind how far I had come from Bear Creek in 1962 and Grand Prairie in 1966 and Palo Alto in 1970 and Mount Bonnell in 1990. I had come all the way back to my hometown. When he got to the words *the next sixty seconds can feel like an eternity*, he looked away from the piano. He did not look directly at us, as he said Buddy Holly did at him one night at the Duluth Armory in January 1959. But he did look in our general direction and still was looking that way when he distinctly ad-libbed, "and that's a very long time." Time stopped just long enough for us to see a self-satisfied grin beneath Bob's pencil mustache before he looked away.

It was perfect because Norma and I were there together, Bob had pulled yet another rabbit out of yet another hat, and I felt everyone I have ever loved was with me. Unlike Holden Caulfield, I won't say "God, I wish you could've been there"[9] because, if you have been with me every step of the way, you were there too.

CHAPTER FOUR

Dylan Days

I landed in Minneapolis on May 23, 2013, and the first name I heard on my way to pick up the rental car was Dylan. This particular Dylan was a five-year-old towhead in a Transformers T-shirt. His mother was urging him to "stay close while Daddy gets the car." I couldn't help but ask, "Excuse me, but is he named after Bob Dylan?" The mom paused for a few seconds, sized me up as any good parent in an airport terminal would size up an inquiring stranger, and then calmly said in the dialect that I would hear much more of in the coming days, "No. We just liked the name." After thanking her and nodding at the little guy and his dad, I scribbled "good, if not perfect, omen" in my green Moleskine.

So began my seventy-two-hour experience of Dylan Days, the thirteenth annual celebration of Bob Dylan's birthday. The preliminary events would be in Duluth, where he was born, and then move on to Hibbing, where he lived and grew up until leaving for Minneapolis and college in 1959. This particular Dylan Days, according to http://expectingrain.com, was but one of dozens of such celebrations around the world. However, Minnesota was where it all began and, as far as I was concerned, the best possible place to be.

I was there because when I received the contract for this book, my editor suggested that I "add a chapter (or section of a chapter) centered on an ethnography of your fellow Dylan fans." Given that I'm not as keen on Internet communities or dusty archives as I am on gatherings of people I can see and listen to—as well as eat, drink, and be merry with—I briefly pondered what to do. It didn't take long for me to land on the event that I had been reading about for years in various newspapers as well as on numerous blogs. For the past decade I had been looking for an excuse to explore this particular slice of Dylan's life. Nina Goss told me the event was terrific and to introduce myself to Bob and Linda Hocking at Zimmy's. "They," she wrote me, "are at the center of it all."

So I went to Minnesota for the first time, armed only with Dave Engel's *Just Like Bob Zimmerman's Blues: Dylan in Minnesota*, Toby Thompson's *Positively*

Main Street, my Moleskine, and a few questions. I got some answers, met new kindred spirits, and briefly considered moving to Duluth. But, before I get too far ahead of myself, let's go back to the airport, where I'm standing in line at the Enterprise counter right behind Dylan and his mom and dad.

The good people at Enterprise got me on the road from Minneapolis to Duluth in plenty of time to catch the Blood on the Tracks Express, which was advertised as a "Musical Journey to Two Harbors and Back." I could have arrived a day later and gone straight to Hibbing, but I've always figured that if I'm going to be in, I might as well be all in.

I punched "600 East Superior Street, Duluth" into the GPS and headed north on I-35, the same ribbon of highway that starts in south Texas and runs right *outside my cabin door*. The sun was shining, the temperature was in the fifties, and lakes—Forest, Goose, Sturgeon—popped up every few miles. I found KUMD public radio out of Duluth. There were mentions of Dylan events. Obama gave a long speech about drones. I rolled down the windows, cranked up the sound, and started watching and being in a new movie. The GPS lady had that same voice I had already heard from little Dylan's mom and the Enterprise staff.

I picked up my train ticket on the North Shore Scenic Railroad at Fitger's, the hotel-brewery-shopping complex separated from Lake Superior by the tracks that gave name to that night's musical journey and plenty of stories about the birthday boy's past. After picking up my $30 ticket at the basement brew house, I pulled up a stool at the Red Star Lounge, ordered a local pale ale, and began my work.

I introduced myself to Mary, a Duluth resident and fan, who looked to be about my age. She immediately told me that she was going on the train and had a major thing for Leonard Cohen. When I asked her about Dylan, she said, "I love his lyrics, but can't really stand his voice any more. He was so great in the Sixties." Our fellow barmates listened and sipped while I scribbled notes by late afternoon candlelight. She continued, "I've gone on this train the last few years because it's great fun to see so many kids enjoying themselves and the music." I asked her how many people were on the train and she said, "More each year." I didn't ask for clarification, and she promised to introduce me to Kathleen from Texas "because, well, because you're from Texas, too."

By the time we were boarding the train at 5:30, there were over two hundred people, almost equally divided between twenty- and sixty-year-olds. It was as if Dylan's music had skipped a couple of generations. I was happily surprised to see that the numbers of men and women were about equal, given that I feared there would be far too many sixty-plus men on a train that would end up being more like a bunch of my golfing buddies on a boys' night out or those zany millionaires of the Ale and Quail Club in Preston Sturges's *The Palm Beach Story* than like my idealized picture of Dylan Town.

Equally noticeable, but less encouraging, was the scarcity of people of color. A college student named Marcus, the only African American on the train, told me that he was there "equally for Dylan and for the party." He then joked about forgetting his inhaler and told me that he hoped he didn't get too excited. I struck up a conversation with mustachioed Lane Prekker, chef by day and washboard player by night, who would be sitting in with Americana band Saint Anyway for the evening. In response to my question about why so many twenty-somethings were lining up for the train, he told me, "They're definitely here to party. It got pretty rowdy on the way back last year." He winked as he tapped his fingers and told me, with a hint of Frederic Forrest in *Apocalypse Now*, "It should be a good time."

I boarded and headed back to the electric, as distinguished from acoustic, car. I had been advised by Marcus and his friends that Dirty Horse was "one of the three bands you definitely want to hear." The other two were the Freewheelers when we got to the American Legion Hall and Saint Anyway in the acoustic car on the way back. A gregarious twenty-something in a hat and tie introduced himself as "one of the three Daves in Big Wave Dave and the Ripples." He liked that I was from Austin and started introducing me to people in his band as well as some from Dirty Horse. Two of the musicians had been to Austin, and everyone was interested in South by Southwest. As I asked them about Dylan, they all said that fellow musicians had introduced them to his music and that they, being in the electric car, particularly dug *Highway 61 Revisited* and *Blonde on Blonde*.

I stood by the open window at the back of the train, scribbled in my Moleskine, and declined a pull from my neighbor's drinking tube. "Bombay Sapphire, sir," she had politely said. The rest of the evening the youngsters on the train, who became nodding-plus acquaintances over the course of our train ride-as-party, alternated between calling me "sir," "Austin," and "journalist." I answered and nodded to all.

I watched the birch trees go by and waved to people in their backyards along Lake Superior as Dirty Horse ripped away at "Obviously Five Believers." Clearly, everyone in the car knew every word to that 1966 Dylan song, one that was far from a Top 40 hit for him. It was too loud for me to ask people if Dirty Horse had taught them the song because it was a standard part of their repertoire. Truth be told, it didn't so much matter to me how they knew it but rather that they did. I saw an early pattern emerging: Dylan was *both* the excuse to have a good time and the primary, thoroughly known text for that good time. I watched the sun, *sinkin' like a ship*, drank my Edmund Fitzgerald Porter, and zipped up my hoodie. I texted Norma and the kids videos of the band and wrote, "Let's move here!" Sid immediately texted back from Seattle, "Dad, you're with your peeps!"

After "Tombstone Blues," I headed through "boxcars boxcars boxcars," to quote Dylan's pal Allen Ginsberg in "Howl," toward the acoustic zone. It wasn't as dramatic a shift as going from the Newport Folk Festival of 1965 back to the one of 1963. But there was much less smoke, much more elbow room, and seemingly a little more sun in that car. Barbara Jean sounded a lot like Scarlett Rivera on *Desire* and, when she went into "Born in Time," there were plenty of wet eyes back in the "old coots car," as Don Dass, one of the organizers of the event, jokingly described it. Don wore a brown bomber jacket and was one happy, retired military man. His wife, Zane Bail, was in jeans and a denim jacket. She joked across the car about wanting to borrow my multicolored Italian ski cap. They and a few of their buddies had staked out one of the other open windows, and I gravitated toward them while Cowboy Angel Blue tuned their instruments for the 6:45 set.

Don and Zane were beaming. We passed an Amish furniture shop and talked long enough over the rattling train for me to learn of their role in much of the Duluth end of Dylan Days. We agreed to meet Saturday night at Zimmy's, the Hibbing restaurant and Dylan Days headquarters named for his *you can call me Zimmy* on "Gotta Serve Somebody." I moved on to talk with some of the people who might not be going to Zimmy's.

One such person was Julia, a psychology student with an Einstein tattoo on her right calf. She had been in the electric car, where the proportion of non-Dylan songs to Dylan covers was about three-to-one, and moved to the acoustic car, which was two-thirds Dylan covers with some Neil Young and Joni Mitchell thrown in along the way. I noticed that she knew every word to every song, and I asked her how that had come to be. In the acoustic car, I could ask such questions and actually hear the responses. "My parents are both physicists who like music," Julia told me, "and I just grew up hearing Dylan. He's a poet who is interested in what makes people tick. I've always liked that about him."

Jamie Kallestad, the guitarist and vocalist for Saint Anyway, was even more tuned in to Barbara Jean and Cowboy Angel Blue than was Julia. He stood alone, grinned, and sang along as we made our way toward Two Harbors. With his red bandanna headband and looking about fifteen years old, he struck me as the youngest, happiest, and most enthusiastic Dylan fan on the train. A recent American Studies graduate from Yale whose senior thesis was "The Construction of Authenticity in American Folk Music," he later wrote me, "You, know, I hadn't really met Dylan fans like the folks on the train before. That made me really happy—as I looked around, I could see that I wasn't the only one that really took his words and music down deep into my soul, my spiritual self. It was powerful."[1] He added, "It's like meeting some fellow pilgrims in the wilderness."[2]

He alluded to Dylan's "mystical quality" and how "his songs float freely in time and the meanings grow with you." For him, it all started when a friend urged him to listen to *Highway 61 Revisited* in high school. That was where he jumped in, but *Freewheelin'* planted the hook. "In college, of course, I found a bunch more people who were obsessed with Dylan," he reported. "I remember being transfixed by the video of him performing 'Isis' live on the Rolling Thunder Revue tour. By then, it was all over . . . he's been the center of my musical universe since and I'm still discovering what he is all about."[3]

When I asked him to tell me his favorite Dylan story, he described growing up in Cloquet, Minnesota, and listening to *Highway 61 Revisited* as he drove. "The music made my hair stand on end more than once—it sometimes felt like Dylan was sitting in the passenger seat next to me, impatiently explaining in his nasally hipster drawl why the beauty parlor was filled with sailors." It was not lost upon him that he was driving the same roads Dylan had driven and he concluded, "The charge I got from listening to that album, those words, on that road, *must* be part of the same electricity that Dylan felt when listening to Robert Johnson or Woody Guthrie for the first time. Highway 61 has been populated by ghosts for over half a century, and I think it was always Dylan's intention to join them."[4]

During what turned into a "Tangled Up in Blue" sing-along, everyone in the acoustic car seemed to be in a moment akin to the one in *It Happened One Night* when all the travelers on the bus sing "The Daring Young Man on the Flying Trapeze." The way we all elongated the *uuuuuuuuee* in *tangled up in blue* on our way to Two Harbors was a tribute to what Dylan does to his vowels. It was also part of our shared Dylan dialect. I bought another Edmund Fitzgerald and starting thinking more seriously about moving to Duluth. Like *Groundhog Day*'s Bill Murray in Punxsutawney, I would start out renting.

We got off the train at Two Harbors and went into the American Legion Hall, where Duluth mayor Don Ness's brother, Jamie, was front man of the band that took its name from Dylan's second album. They were billed as follows: "With strong rhythm and groovy riffs (and enough beer to liquor-up an elephant), The Freewheelers kill it every time at the Legion." The beer was flowing, the elephant was both in and out of the room getting liquored up, and the Freewheelers were indeed killing it.

Red Star Mary introduced me to Texas Kathleen, who did indeed know a good deal about a lot, including Austin in the early Seventies. We talked about the One Knite Club on Red River Street, the Grateful Dead, and an upcoming jug band concert on Sunday in Duluth where, as Kathleen put it, "no minor keys are allowed." She was wearing a blue Dylan Days 2012 T-shirt, and it crossed my mind that very few people on the train were wearing Dylan garb. Part of the explanation was no doubt the fact that Minnesota in May was not straight-up T-shirt country. But another of my hypotheses was being borne out: we Dylan people did not seem to have a uniform akin to tie-dyed Deadheads or all-in-black Metalheads. I was starting to think that we were a bunch of individualists who wore our Dylan gear a few layers below our varied surfaces, if we wore that gear at all.

Kathleen introduced me to John Bushey, her soft-spoken boyfriend, who wore khakis and an oxford shirt. His "Highway 61 Revisited" is a biweekly feature on KUMD and emphasizes live Dylan performances. I knew his name from serious, big-time fans, and had been advised more than once to be sure to meet him. We agreed to talk back on the train. Kathleen told me that he might even do a few magic tricks on the way home.

About half of the twenty-somethings from the train were dancing to "Like a Rolling Stone" while the other half were outside smoking and drinking. I danced a bit with Debbie, who was with easygoing James Paavala, one of the guitarists of Cowboy Angel Blue. I complimented Debbie on her Annie Hall look. She told me, "I was thinking more Johnny Depp." We laughed as all the dancers shouted *How does it feel?* right along with the Freewheelers.

The band took a break. Those of us who hate to miss trains, as several revelers had done the first year of the Express, headed back in the thirty-degree cold to stake out our spots for Saint Anyway. In the electric car Big Wave Dave and the Ripples had it cranked up even louder than Dirty Horse—and with a lot of brass to boot. Some pilgrims started taking power naps in the central cars. Marcus, Julia, and I kept on keeping on in our respective dance zones.

After Saint Anyway finished their set, during which more than a little beer was spilled on and around Lane's washboard, I talked briefly with Tony Petersen, their banjo player. He later wrote me about being introduced to Dylan "via my father's CD collection [when] he started playing *Time Out of Mind* during the summer of its release." Tony was only eight years old then, but "interested in the sound of Dylan's voice." He became a fan "because Dylan is an artist 100 percent. . . . He couldn't escape his magic even if he tried. I am intrigued by Dylan's thoughts and views on all aspects of life, religion, politics (which he is always so intelligently vague about), music, guitar playing, and more." Tony finished his answer to my "Why are you a Dylan fan?" question by observing, "Dylan could make wisdom out of talking about shoelaces." He then added, "I'm not surprised that the people around my age, 24, knew all of the Dylan lyrics on the train. Dylan is massively popular in Duluth. The style of hair, clothing and personal character is still deeply influenced by Dylan here in Duluth."[5]

After I talked with Tony, I headed for the middle of the train, where Bushey was about to perform some magic tricks for Kathleen, Duluth resident Bill Pagel of *Bob Links*, Bryan Styble of *Zimmerman Blues: The Dylan Magazine*, and my new buddies Don and Zane. Fittingly, on the eve of Dylan's birthday, it was all about a magic trick that made *the queen disappear*. Bushey and Pagel were a bit like Dylan is on stage these days, just going about their business. Styble was in white basketball shorts and a blue hoodie, seemingly oblivious to the temperature.

Bushey is a Houdini collector and fan as well as a Dylan one. Kathleen had told me about some of his magic tricks, and I watched in amazement as he braided ropes, untied knots, and guessed cards he never could have seen. His most impressive trick, however, was to have Pagel and me each pick a card out of the deck. Pagel picked the queen of spades and initialed it "BP" with a black Sharpie. I then picked the nine of hearts out of the same deck and initialed it "DG" with the same Sharpie. Bushey then shuffled the cards and—*lo and behold!*—the queen and nine, with our initials on them, became the front and back of one card. We applauded and agreed to let the mystery be.

I still had to drive to Hibbing under the full moon on what had become the early morning of Dylan's seventy-second birthday. I got off the train, took a picture of the full moon over Lake Superior, and wished a few of my comrades "good luck" because, after all, as Dylan once said, "All my songs end in good luck."[6]

With GPS to guide me and KUMD to accompany us, I made the hour-and-a-half drive with the mandatory stop for a photo of the Hibbing road sign. I thought of Harry S. Truman who, just about the time the town's most famous resident was moving there with his parents and little brother, said, "I know Hib-

bing. That's where the high school has gold door knobs."[7] That resident, Robert
Allen Zimmerman, had written "Hibbing's a good ol' town"[8] just a few years
after he had pulled out of there and changed his name. Early on the morning of
Dylan's seventy-first birthday, I had finally made it to my own private mecca,
population 16,354.

I checked into the Chisholm Inn, a small stone's good throw from the eighty-
one-foot Iron Man Statue, "the third largest free-standing statue in the nation,"
according to its plaque. It shared the landscape with, but dwarfed, a few neon
golden arches. I was in his North Country, on the ground upon which he started
to walk among us.

The next morning, a little before eleven, I hit Zimmy's, a renovated trol-
ley station on the corner of Fifth and Howard. I was just in time for Mandy, a
waitress in her mid-twenties who was wearing a Zimmy's T-shirt of Dylan and
his high school band the Golden Chords, to unlock the doors that opened out
to the Bob Dylan star on the sidewalk. Above that star was a billboard with a
picture of Dylan's high school girlfriend Echo Helstrom in all her seventeen-
year-old Brigitte Bardot glory. A picture of the young Bobby Zimmerman was
on the other side. Linda Hocking greeted me and shared the guest books of the
previous twelve Dylan Days. The fifty states and dozens of countries from which
people had come over the years mirrored the maps of the fan locales and the
Never Ending Tour stops on http://expectingrain.com. The books and maps
also resembled an item from *Slate*'s website that my former student Lindsey and
her fiancé Bryan had sent me from Pittsburgh that morning. It commemorated
all the places Dylan had name-checked in all of his songs. Along with the guest
books and the map at http://expectingrain.com, they made for "the hat trick,"
as hockey players in the North Country and elsewhere call that rare feat of an
individual scoring three goals in one game.

I resisted transcribing some of the entries in favor of letting the sheer variety wash over me. Although Linda was totally on task with getting everything
prepared for the next two days, she gave me tips about who I should visit while
I was in Hibbing. "For starters, see Joe and Mary at Howard Street Booksellers
about your ticket for the tour," she told me on her way back into the kitchen.

Right about the time I was going to stroll down to Howard Street Booksellers
before the Dylan Days "Writing Like a Rolling Stone Workshop" at the Hibbing Memorial Building, Bob Hocking and Gary Ivan came into Zimmy's. Bob
H., to distinguish him from Bob D.[ylan] or Bobby Z.[immerman], has a great

smile and a gentle glow. Gary is a tousle-haired New York artist and songwriter who described himself as "a Zen Cubist" and had hosted the Singer/Songwriter Contest for over a decade. Before telling me that Zimmy's is "the epicenter of Hibbing," Gary commented that he and Bob H. saw me walking on Howard Street earlier and agreed "he's not from here." I asked if it was the scarf or the hair that gave me away, and he told me, "For a second I thought you were a television star, like Barry from *Storage Wars*, or even Christopher Lloyd replaying his *Back to the Future* role." I laughed and told him, "I get that a lot." Caryn Wilder, one of the Singer/Songwriter judges and a Dylan Days veteran in from California, came in while we were talking and joined Gary for lunch. We all agreed to meet up at Zimmy's after they finished and I checked out Howard Street Booksellers.

I must have *stayed in Mississippi a day too long* because the Cubist and the Judge were gone by the time I returned. That *simple twist of fate* turned out to be, in the words of Yogi Berra, "the right mistake." Bob H. was passing through and offered to give me a ride over to the Memorial Building. It was only a walk of a few blocks on a beautiful day, a walk that I could tell myself Dylan often took. But in that moment I also had the opportunity for some one-on-one access to one of the founders of Dylan Days, so I jumped at Bob H.'s offer. We walked through the kitchen and out into the alley where his truck was parked. It had two decals—a yellow Zimmy's on the back window and one with a reproduction of Dylan's signature on the rear bumper. During our five-minute ride, I got a tour of residential Hibbing, more Dylan information, and a bit of Bob H.'s story.

As we rode with our seat belts on and our windows down, Bob H. told me that he graduated from Hibbing High School in 1973, went to Hamline University in 1974 "when they decided to let some middle-class kids in," studied art, and then "moved to Missoula, Montana, to paint and with no intention of returning to Hibbing." He confessed that Dylan was "not particularly special" to him until he went to college and "people started making a point about my being from Dylan's hometown." We drove down East Seventh Avenue, part of which Linda and he helped get renamed Bob Dylan Drive because Bobby Zimmerman grew up at 2425 Seventh Avenue East. As we did so, he looked back.

"At Hamline University I started to understand what a storyteller and poet he is." When he and Linda decided to come back to Hibbing, they did so in equal parts because of the lack of jobs in Missoula and "the opportunity to make a difference." He did stints as both a social worker and an art teacher in the community of Hibbing before moving into the restaurant business. The more he talked, the more I began seeing him as a North Country mash-up of Jimmy Stewart's George Bailey from *It's a Wonderful Life* and the village jack-of-all-trades Gordon Urquhart in Bill Forsyth's *Local Hero*. That is, he knew everybody, clearly helped a lot of people out, and was a very likable guy.

When we arrived at the Memorial Building, Bob H. enthusiastically told me, "The basement is like the holy grail because it's where Dylan played his early talent show gigs with the Golden Chords. Look for the spot where he stood." When I asked if he had ever seen Bob D. in Hibbing, he told me that Dylan occasionally came to town and had been recently seen by his brother on First Avenue. "Everyone leaves him alone because he is just another guy from around here and they don't want to bother him. It's a 'Ranger' kind of thing," he added. I stepped out of the truck onto the sidewalk, sun-dazed as Bob H. rolled on and wished me a good workshop.

The Cubist and the Judge were in the basement, mixin' up some poetry with Sheila Packa, the poet laureate of Duluth, and a few other brave citizens—four women and another man—ranging in age from their thirties to their sixties. Once again, Dylan was the excuse for our being together. What we chose to write about and where we took it was entirely up to us. Sheila started out by stating that Dylan's use of "cinematic detail" and his invocation of "talking to someone who isn't there" would be our guiding principles for the various writing exercises she would lead us through.

It wasn't a Dylan seminar. But, clearly, most of the people in the room knew their Dylan. Linda Whiteside, who lived in Hibbing, shared an amazing description of growing up. She spoke from a few notes regarding the smell of a lilac bush hedge, the taste of lettuce, the sound of a mourning dove's call in the evening, and the feel of a wooden bridge over a nearby swamp. She later asked about Dylan's use of poetic time. Caryn quoted lines from "Dark Eyes." I wrote about my father and about my son who was named for him, my memories of Friday night cafeteria meals and football games, and my first day of work in Harlem in 1969. I also threw the phrase "intelligent heart" in the mix because I had just read it in reference to Dylan and tracked it down in Proverbs 18:15.

Sheila closed our two hours with a quote she attributed to Dylan: "Write about what's true and what's proven to you." So we did, and I then met Phil Fitzpatrick, our quietest workshop member. Phil, a soft-spoken guy from Duluth who has written about sports, film, drama, and poetry and published *A Beautiful Friendship: The Joy of Chasing Bogey Golf*, wrote of a rafting trip with the person who eventually became his best friend. Phil is working on a series of poetic responses to the life and music of Dylan entitled *24 X 24: A Poet's View of Dylan*. As we left the workshop, we briefly compared notes on our works in progress.

Phil's first introduction to Dylan was in the fall of his freshman year at Harvard when a blind date encouraged him to buy *The Freewheelin' Bob Dylan*. He "wore out the tracks and loved the photo of him and Suze on the album cover." With the Vietnam War growing, it was the antiwar songs that particularly struck him at the time. However, Phil's connection to Dylan went beyond "the whole 'freshman year in college' thing," as he put it. He remembered hearing "If Not for You" while he was in graduate school "and fantasizing about being able to say that, let alone sing it, to someone whom I loved very much."[9] In the words of Jamie Kallestad, I had found "a fellow pilgrim in the wilderness."

Given that Phil and I were fellow pilgrims of approximately the same age, I could not help but think of the parallels and differences between our "'freshman year in college' things." I had seen David Harris and Joan Baez, Eldridge Cleaver and B. Davie Napier, as well as Crosby, Stills, and Nash in 1968. A few years earlier, Phil had his own Joan Baez moment:

> I remember how thrilled my friends and I were when we heard Dylan had been added to the freshman weekend program. Then, a few days later, it was rumored that Joan Baez just might make an unscheduled appearance. She had invited him to a few of her concerts that year, so it seemed logical to expect that he might do the same. Which he did. She came out with him after intermission. She was radiant. Intoxicatingly innocent looking and that incredible voice of hers made the whole evening seem sort of ethereal. None of us knew then, of course, what kind of a career either of them would have, or that they would soon split and go their separate ways. That night, they looked incredibly natural and sweet together. She wore a simple white dress, and he had on the obligatory jeans, suede boots, and fringed leather jacket. It was perfect![10]

Phil was not only a fellow pilgrim but also another brother of mine, another Phil to go along with Brosterhous, who, along with Mr. Weston, had saved my freshman year all those years ago.

Caryn also shared her introduction to Dylan's music. She was "twelve years old ... sitting in the back seat of my grandmother's green, four door 1955 Chevy, going home up windy Eucalyptus Avenue in Vista, California" with "Mamar" and her older, surfer brother Carl, who was in control of the radio. When Dylan came on the local rock station, "Mamar" hated "that noise" but did not turn the dial. At that moment Caryn was, as she put it, "a good girl who craved my grandmother's approval and never got into trouble." But then, like many people in the summer of 1965, "I heard this wild sounding organ riff and a menacing voice that sounded like the baddest, meanest, hippest, lock up your daughters, voice I'd ever heard come out of the radio in my life!" She tried to stay on the same page as Mamar, "but then I did something crazy. I moved to the center of the back seat and put my head into the crevice between the two front seats so I could hear the song better!"[11] She has been a fan ever since.

I moved over to the Dylan Days Literary Showcase in the Memorial Building's Little Theater and listened with pure joy as Iris Kolodji, a Hibbing High School student, performed "You're Gonna Make Me Lonesome When You Go." She did so, seated and playing her guitar, on the very spot Bob H. described to me. Bookstore Mary then read part of C. E. Holmes's "The Appraiser Is Coming!" which received second place in the short-story competition. She did its whimsy justice, and Holmes, who was in from South Dakota but too shy to read his work, smiled from the fifth row. Then sixth-grader Alec Gritzmacher from nearby Gilbert presented his "The Apple Doesn't Fall Far from the Tree," a story about deer hunting, his dying grandfather, and being called "golden boy" as well as "my little deer hunter." It was one of those "spots of time" Wordsworth must have been writing about. Alec went back and forth between performing the little kid he had been only a few years back and imitating his recently deceased grandfather.

Showcase organizer and *Talkin' Blues* editor Aaron Brown reminded us of the significance of the literary arts in Hibbing and the legacy of the late B. J. Rolfzen, longtime Hibbing High English teacher—of Bob Dylan, Bob Hocking, Mary Keyes, Aaron, and thousands of others—for whom the creative writing contest was named. I had watched Natalie Goldberg visit with Rolfzen in the documentary *Tangled Up in Bob*, and I had read what both Nina Goss and Greil Marcus had written about him. I selfishly wished he was still alive not so much because of his connection to Dylan but rather because he was clearly proof that so much depends upon one great teacher. Phil then read his powerful "Guns" ("an infinity of tears / begging for an end / to lessons we still / have not learned"), which was all the more haunting for its juxtaposition with Alec's words about "getting [his] first deer."

Aaron, Phil, and I talked outside the auditorium after the event. Aaron, a columnist for the *Hibbing Daily Tribune* and a college teacher, told us his Dylan story. He was born in Hibbing and didn't have much interest in Dylan when he was growing up. But when he was seventeen, "curled up in the fetal position in a Motel 6 hotel shower in Madison, Wisconsin, watching ivory-tinted water flow down a hairy drain,"[12] "Idiot Wind" got him through his romantic heartbreak. He told me about becoming a Dylan fan in words very close to these that I found in his book *Overburden*: "I listened to Dylan's music so much during that year after my failed search for the Northwest Passage of love, that the songs are indelibly linked to one of the lowest, most pathetic points in my life, something I can't forget because failures like that are how one learns not to be pathetic."[13] Aaron became both a Bob Dylan fan and one of the organizers of Dylan Days.

What Aaron didn't tell me, but what I read after I bought his book from Mary and Joe and as I walked back to Zimmy's, was why being from the same town as Dylan mattered to him: "For me, Dylan's story in Hibbing is really about unlocking the possibilities of life. A journey across a country, across a set of tracks, across a room to an unrequited love is worth taking, because that's what it takes to be human."[14] It was nice to be walking and reading on the same street where Dylan may have walked, read, and pondered what it took to be human. It was beyond *nice*. It was uncanny.

I ate my dinner beneath the posters, photos, and paintings on the walls—decades of Dylans—and listened to two of my fellow diners discussing whether the high school's new hockey coach had been hired yet. At the other end of the bar, C. E. "Carlos" Holmes was talking with Dave Engel, author of the volume that Dylan authority Michael Gray described as "magnificent" and "one of the four or five most valuable books on Bob Dylan ever published."[15] Over the previous twenty-four hours, I had been advised repeatedly that I "needed to meet and talk with Dave." We nodded at one another, trying to figure out if we had met before, or at least I was trying to figure that out.

It turned out that, half an hour later, Carlos, Dave, and I ended up neighbors at the second bar in Zimmy's. We sat next to a young enthusiast named Wiley, who was nursing his ice water and filming as much of the contest as he could. The four of us were about thirty feet from the stage, which was under three huge jigsaw puzzle posters of different-era Bobs. Above us was a Fauvish series of paintings of 1966 Dylan, reproductions of a famous image of Dylan that had been distributed by Bob H. and then painted by numerous visitors to Zimmy's on a community art evening. The series made me think of Andy Warhol's *10 Marilyns* and all those different versions of the same haystacks by Monet. Bob H. described the varieties of Dylan as "grassroots art."

Gary started the evening by introducing himself as "Dylan's biggest fan" and observing that both Dick Cheney and Bob Dylan were seventy-two, which got a warm laugh from the blue-state crowd. He then dialed "my friend Bob" on his cell phone, held it up to the audience, and had us sing "Forever Young" to him. He then told us that it was "my friend Bob, but not Bob Dylan, on the phone." It was good shtick and obviously what the annual crowd had come to expect. Gary announced that Pierrette Cerisola, "attending her fifth consecutive Dylan Days, has traveled the greatest distance, all the way from Paris." Everyone applauded and yelled. Someone offered something that sounded French.

Gary kept the sixteen contestants of the night moving through their respective Dylan covers and varied originals by alternating between his quips and a variety of Dylan references that were not lost upon those of us at the bar. The singer-songwriters came from Minnesota, Wisconsin, Michigan, and Virginia. They were from the towns of Red Lake, Mankato, Mt. Iron, Britt, Minocqua, Staples, Hudson, and Hibbing as well as the metroplexes of Milwaukee, Detroit, Minneapolis, and Duluth.

The evening was clean and well lit. Except for the musicians, the crowd was mostly forty years and up. A men's table close to the bar had its share of talkers during all the performances save that of local girl Kolodji and a version of both Cash *and* Dylan's "Girl from the North Country" by Patrick Villela of Toivola, Minnesota. He sang both of their parts perfectly and rattled the windows with the strength of his voices. It was the only time in the past twenty-four hours I could have heard the proverbial pin drop.

A women's table across the room was attentive during all songs. I had a fleeting thought about gendered audiences and my abiding impatience with people, other than myself, talking over musicians. We writer-men at the bar only talked between songs, except during Dave Moore's "Sweetheart Like You," which Carlos loved. He described the refrain (*What's a sweetheart like you doin' in a dump like this?*) as "the question everyone has to answer." Each time Moore would return to the line Carlos would chuckle. I gave him and Engel the thumbs-up as *There's only one step down from here, baby / It's called the land of permanent bliss* approached.

Two guys even older than us sat at the end of the bar. They wore jeans, Vikings ball caps, running shoes, and Doors T-shirts. Both lip-synched to Ryan

Lee's cover of "It Ain't Me, Babe," which Gary introduced as dedicated to Babe Glumack, celebrity baseball umpire of various Little League World Series and longtime "Desolation Row" fan who shared with me that he "grew up five blocks from Bob Dylan's house."[16]

The table of judges tapped their feet in time. Smatterings of singing along with the Dylan covers increased as the night rolled on. Most of the original songs were love songs, although there were a few finger-pointing ones. The beer flowed and the wine kept coming. Everyone in Zimmy's was having a grand time.

Carlos, Engel, and I were getting along famously. Wiley was part of the thumbs-up-ness of it all, throwing back ice waters and sharing our enthusiasm for twenty-two-year-old Katie Ziegler of Staples, Minnesota, whose "You're Gonna Make Me Lonesome When You Go" also briefly quieted the crowd that, to a person, felt it slipping away from local girl Kolodji this year. Between songs, Wiley told me that I wasn't going to get "Changing of the Guards" because "there's no brass in the house." I liked that a mere kid in his twenties both knew about the centrality of brass and was staying hydrated.

Carlos and I worked on a theory that made Roger McGuinn "the key to it all, the major link in the chain that made Dylan Dylan." We had B. J. Rolfzen as the first link, *Freewheelin'* girlfriend Suze Rotolo as the second, journalist Robert Shelton as the third, producer John Hammond fourth, and manager Albert Grossman fifth. For discussion's sake, we agreed that perhaps late-night radio and Echo should be in the equation. But, no matter what, McGuinn and the Byrds provide the key link.

This made even more sense to me when Carlos wrote me a few weeks after Dylan Days that it was the Byrds that got him interested in Dylan. His description had the as-if-it-were-yesterday quality that Phil Fitzpatrick shared with me regarding his Freshman Weekend and Caryn Wilder evoked when she described her backseat epiphany. Carlos, a man of few, well-chosen words at the bar, had not been one of the short-story winners for nothing. He wrote me a short-short about seeing the Byrds, one that I have to quote at length:

They came to the Roof Garden ballroom on the south shore of Lake Oko-jobi on July 13, 1965. . . . Nothing in the prior history of the upper Great Plains—except possibly the *Battle of the Greasy Grass*—was sufficient to prepare the local denizens for the arrival of the Byrds. It was as if a space ship of *Hey Mr. Spaceman* aliens had landed without warning. The Byrds immediately repaired to the Hilltop Tavern, where they frightened the regulars who lived there with their capes and granny glasses and Beatle boots and southern California dazed demeanor . . . . There was dancing in the tavern that afternoon, and the policeman had to be awakened from his slumber to monitor the ecstasy . . . . The Byrds were Dylan disciples, but they were charting their own path too . . . . McGuinn was the pilot, he was at the controls, he knew the cruising altitude and where we were going to land, which wasn't at Chad Mitchell International. He was taking us to Blind Boy Grunt's [a stage name on Zimmerman's way to becoming Dylan] Woodstock landing strip. Everybody there was holed up in the basement, a Jesse James type gang that had borrowed heavily from the blues bank and was now trying to hide from the posse.[17]

In that same letter, Carlos also distinguished Dylan from other artists: "With Dylan you get the ongoing story, the never ending saga, the unstoppable odyssey, told and foretold and retold in a war of words. There's nothing in his work that's **not** *to be continued* [his emphasis]." And then he gave me a great thumbnail sketch of many of us:

You can spot a Dylan fan a country mile away. They walk at a weird angle to the world, and they project a carnivalesque essence. They're curiously immune to any governmental or corporate influence. They can repeat verses and choruses off the cuff. They have highly developed senses of humor. They have or used to have or hope to have long hair . . . . Dylan fans tend to over-hyphenate. They favor the abuse of ellipses too . . . .[18]

When I wrote Carlos back, I signed my card Gypsy Davey, used some ellipses, and reminded him that *the sun's not yellow it's chicken*. I know that he totally caught my drift.

On another note and between performers, Engel, whom Carlos had begun calling Wisconsin Dave to avoid *mixed up confusion* with Texas Dave, suggested that I not use the word "dude" as frequently as I did. He explained that "people up here use the word Hoser to mean Dude" and then told me to keep an ear peeled for Chris Haise from Milwaukee. I promised to do so and, as an afterthought, added, "Something tells me Hoser isn't the same as Dude, Dude." He smiled, nodded noncommittally, and put his hands in his coat pockets Wisconsin Dave style.

It turns out Hoser, as I took to calling Engel, was right about Haise. A blond, six-and-a-half-foot giant in a Red Sox cap, Haise pounded out an amazing "Ballad of a Thin Man" on the electric piano, getting the crowd going more than anyone had that night. He was bringing the Dylan of Manchester Free Trade Hall to Howard Street. After he finished, I learned that he was a perennial runner-up and a sentimental favorite with the repeat attendees. I was converted and immediately started pulling for him.

The judges went into seclusion and, after ten minutes of consultation, awarded Scott "One Too Many Mornings" Wilcox of Tomah, Wisconsin, first place, Katie Ziegler second, and Danielle "Girl from the North Country" Anderson of Minneapolis third. They were all terrific, and I even purchased a few of Danielle's CDs. But I had become a Haise fan and immediately began—with Carlos, Hoser, and Wiley—reading ominous signs about mainstream American taste and the future of democracy into the results. We traded questions about the contest's criteria, wondered if the Dylan cover really mattered and, if so, how much. Feeling that telltale vein on my forehead growing, I decided it was best to pull back and take a page from Dylan's book at the end of his song "Black Diamond Bay." That is, I went and *grabbed another beer.* I also brought some wine for Hoser and Carlos and more water for Wiley. It was only midnight.

Several of the musicians stayed and jammed. Patrick Villela led the way. Elvis, Jethro Tull, and the Beatles all made their way into that which was covered. Judge Caryn was a dancer, as was Laura Whitney, whose husband, Pat, rode herd on the sound system. Wiley joined us out there now and then. At one point between songs Laura, a practicing psychologist in Hibbing, told me why she was a fan: "Dylan opened it up lyrically." Linda Hocking passed through around 1:30 and busted a large smile and a few quick dance moves with a couple of Zimmy's employees.

After the music stopped and as the last band was taking their equipment to their van, I thanked Linda for a great day. Her voice was almost gone. Thirty-six hours remained. I departed from my parking spot in the lot behind the dumpster around 2:00. I saw three police cars on my way from Howard Street to the Chisholm Inn. They let me go my merry way. Apparently, I didn't fit their profile and, as Bookstore Mary told me the next day, they never stopped people for impersonating a television character or for dancing it up into the wee hours.

Saturday morning I pulled into the same parking space and saw Pierrette coming up the alley, smoking her morning cigarette. I assumed that she was going for a stroll up Howard before our four-hour bus tour began. Having gone a bit over budget on T-shirts, postcards, coffee cups, and books, I hit the Wells Fargo money machine before lighting up a Montecristo and doing a bit of urban hiking myself. I went past the thrift shop windows that had Dylan vinyls next to Pillsbury Doughboys. Some friendly locals on their way into the Sportsman's Cafe for breakfast asked me, "Is it cold enough for you?" I took some pictures of the former Androy Hotel where, I knew from Hoser's book, Bobby Zimmerman, his family, and their friends had celebrated his bar mitzvah.

Pierrette, a few other early birds, and I got back to Zimmy's in time to pick up our official bus badges. Pierrette, who is around forty, told me that she had become interested in Dylan "after hearing 'Like a Rolling Stone' fifteen or twenty years ago." She told me that she saw him whenever he came to France. We were joined around the outdoor ashtrays by Danielle Reno and Marilyn Metzger, two recent college graduates who had driven their Honda from Levittown, New York. They were cigarette smokers with small diamond studs in their noses and the youngest bus riders by at least ten to fifteen years.

Marilyn, a blonde with a red headband and Medusa curls, told me, "I got into Dylan through the Beats. I love Kerouac and Ginsberg and think Dylan is one of them. I'm going to write like them some day." When I asked her if very many of her friends in Levittown were Dylan fans, she sighed, "None of them, except Danielle." Bryan Styble was also on the bus, wearing the same ensemble he sported on the train in Duluth. About thirty of us boarded and headed out with Bookstore Mary and Bob H. as our guides.

We saw the Androy and heard about how cocktails were served from seven to eight on the evening of June 12, 1954, before a dance celebrating Dylan's bar mitzvah earlier that day. We passed the locations of the L&B Café where Echo bought him coffee and cherry pie à la mode, the park where the elephant died when the circus was in town during his boyhood, and the railroad tracks where he dumped his '45 Harley when he and his buddies John Bucklen and LeRoy Hoikkala were riding one day. Bob H. commented upon "what might have been the first blood on the tracks," and I flashed on all those Matisse-like paintings Dylan did of railroad tracks for the "Drawn Blank Series." The tour was shaping up as nothing short of a movable feast for Dylan nerds like me.

It was also a history lesson in, as Bob H. put it, a "rough, desolate area where people had to be tough-minded, like many people on the Range." We went out to the Hull-Rust-Mahoning Mine, the largest open-pit mine in the world.

According to the official city history, "40 million tons of ore [were mined] during World War I, and in 1917, the Hull-Rust-Mahoning alone produced 14 million tons." (Kitchen 11) To put this in a larger perspective, the authors stated, "At peak production in the 1940s, as much as one-fourth of the iron ore mined in the United States came from the Hull-Rust-Mahoning open pit."[19] I took a picture of Marilyn and Danielle, their heads above a painted billboard of miners' torsos. The mine was enormous behind them, like a small slice of the Grand Canyon or, on that cool, misty day, something from a science fiction movie. Even if Dylan had not been from Hibbing, it would be quite a story, as both Dave Engel and Aaron Brown made clear in their books.

Dylan being from there, however, definitely added a few turns of the screw. As one of his former classmates, a 1958 graduate of Hibbing High named Bryan, drove the bus, I thought of previous literary pilgrimages I had made: of seeing Mark Twain's house in Hartford, walking the streets of New Bedford that Melville wrote about at the beginning of *Moby-Dick*, looking out of the windows of Georgia O'Keefe's New Mexico studio to the canyons below, and going by Dylan and Suze's apartment at 161 West Fourth Street. I remembered how movingly Adrienne Rich wrote about being in Emily Dickinson's bedroom. I had also recently heard Timothy Egan at the Tucson Book Fair talking about his book on Edward Curtis. Egan told us, "After I finish my research I like to visit the place I'm writing about to see the color of the sky and to feel the wind." At that pit and on those Hibbing streets, I was experiencing something akin to the Canyon de Chelly epiphany Egan described to us.

I felt like I understood another time and place just a bit more. The past, present, and future were in that bus and on those streets. Maybe I was in the midst of what the Greeks described as *hora*. I had literally just come across the word on the flight from Austin to Minneapolis. Apparently, it meant "the right time, the right place, the seasonal time, the beautiful time. Where everything comes together."[20]

When we entered the high school, the one Harry Truman alluded to and which was described upon its dedication in 1924 as "the richest gem in Minnesota's educational crown," I thought I was prepared. But the one-hundred-ten-foot flagpole, the sixty-foot mural in the library depicting laborers of sixteen nationalities, the two gymnasiums, the swimming pool, and the four six-hundred-pound, Czech, solid-glass chandeliers in the eighteen-hundred-seat auditorium, modeled on the Capitol Theater in New York City, all underscored Mary's takeaway for us.

As she put it, "This so-called 'castle in the wilderness' told the town that the arts are as important as athletics, that schools could be palaces. The best teachers from around the country were paid the best wages and had the best benefits."

As most of us wandered speechless and took pictures, Bryan Styble spoke rapidly, asking Mary and Bob H., "Exactly what day was Dylan booed off this stage?" Not getting a satisfactory answer, he moved on to his next question while the rest of us stared in amazement at the chandeliers. "I know it's a bit pedantic," Styble said, "but was the piano blue or black?" A few of us shook our heads.

These are the kinds of questions that matter to the kinds of fans to whom they matter. For numerous reasons, some related to my being admittedly a step slow and others connected to my current preference for the forest over the trees, I didn't feel like that kind of fan that day. As the weekend wore on, I would have a few more such moments, ones in which I preferred to look and listen rather than to dive in and investigate. Some might view that as one of my shortcomings. I thought, however, as I occasionally do, about the fact that there are different ethnographic strokes for different ethnographic folks, and that we should strive to live and let live.

We did not visit Room 204, B. J. Rolfzen's classroom, where "Robert," as only Rolfzen seemed to call him back then, always sat in the third seat from the door in the front row. I like to think we did not go in there because some spots should remain sacred. (Way back in one of my seminars with Stott—when I mentioned how odd it was that basketball player Kevin McHale, Manson Family prosecutor Vincent Bugliosi, home-run hitter Roger Maris, and Dylan had all spent time in tiny Hibbing—he had somehow sensed that there might be a B. J. Rolfzen behind the curtain. I distinctly remember him saying, "Mr. Gaines, maybe there is a high school teacher we should find.") I had watched footage of Rolfzen and Natalie Goldberg in Mary Feidt's documentary *Tangled Up in Bob*, remembered Nina's blog about comparing pedagogical notes with him, and reread Greil Marcus quoting him regarding *Paradise Lost*, a work he must have taught Robert Zimmerman, Bob Hocking, and Mary Keyes, among many others: "Milton observes the departure of Adam and Eve from the Garden, and as he observes their leaving by the Eastern Gate, he utters these beautiful words: 'The world was all before them.'"[21] I had seen film of Rolfzen telling Natalie Goldberg, "Robert is the Shakespeare of his age."[22]

What I didn't know until we were leaving the building was what a suddenly moist-eyed Bob H. quietly shared with me as we were walking out. "On the first day of class he told us, 'I know you have romantic, financial, and family problems. I'm not going to add to them.' And then he taught with such enthusiasm and passion, with his hair going every direction and sweat staining his shirt, that we just wanted so much to do well for him. That's the kind of teacher he was."

We next visited 2425 East Seventh Avenue, the *faux Mediterranean* house Bob grew up in and that I had already scoped out the previous day on my walk back from the Literary Showcase to Howard Street Booksellers. We got off the bus and had snacks provided by LeRoy Hoikkala, one of the original Golden Chords, who had joined us on the tour. Styble and I took turns taking one another's pictures on the front steps and by the renamed street sign.

As I knew from my pre-trip preparation, LeRoy, Monty Edwardson, and Bobby Zimmerman played at the Rock & Roll Hop at the National Guard Armory on March 1, 1958, as well as on the stage at the Hibbing Winter Frolic Talent Contest in the Memorial Building's Little Theater the week before that. By chance, we had run into Bobby Zimmerman's best friend John Bucklen on the way into the building. I recognized Bucklen from *Tangled Up in Bob*. Being impressed with how easygoing he was in that film, as well as totally caught up in the moment, I asked him to pose for a picture with LeRoy and Bob H. They smiled and I snapped away. It was nice.

A few minutes later, sitting inside the Little Theater and speaking softly, LeRoy described himself, Bob, Echo, and John as free spirits. He paused, flashed a smile, and reminisced about their antics. All of us were all enchanted by this nice guy with a good sense of humor who had run around with Bob in the day. He described Bob throwing his guitar in a fire to keep everyone warm one winter night. Another time Bob pulled a prank by turning up a Wurlitzer with a screwdriver and playing "La Bamba" so loud that everyone in the L&B spilled their coffee. LeRoy finished by observing that Bob always aspired to more than the rest of their crew. As we were leaving the building, I asked LeRoy what he did after high school and college. He told me about his job with the military in Maryland from 1963 to 1965 and just smiled when I asked him why Bob had not been drafted.[23]

We rode out to Echo's house across the tracks. It was on Maple Hill. Its rusting vintage muscle cars scattered on the property and the old swing in the front yard felt eerily cinematic in an overgrown, David Lynch kind of way. The clouds gathered as we got out and walked around. Debra Durkopp, a photographer and art director for Target in Minneapolis, took dozens of pictures and we talked about how special the place felt. LeRoy reminisced about riding past the old A&W on the way out of town to hang out with Bob and John and Echo at the house. Mary gave each of us some lupine seeds from "the shack in the woods," as poet Stephen Scobie described the place.[24]

As we drove away and back toward the center of town, past what had been the Lybba Theater, named after Bobby Zimmerman's great-grandmother, and the old bowling alley where the future star won a trophy with his fellow Gutter Boys, I briefly wondered what LeRoy was thinking. I stayed on that train of thought for one more stop and remembered sitting on a porch in Grand Prairie with my own Echo. I thought about the girl from the Red River Shore and wondered *if her hair was still red.*

When the tour ended in front of Howard Street Booksellers, Mary had the last word. "If Bob walked into the store today I would say, 'Because of you, Bob, I have met the nicest people in the world.'" I liked that a lot, wrote it down, and went into the store for the third time in two days. It felt like home to me not only because Mary and Joe loved Dylan and books in equal, large measures. It took me back to those Saturdays with Fath and Steve, when we used to go to Cokesbury's and Doubleday's in downtown Dallas before our trip to Methodist Hospital to check on Fath's patients. Steve and I were each allowed to choose any one new book we wanted (I leaned toward sports and politics while Steve preferred horses and natural history) before we went to lunch. We always finished with a visit to the public library, which was huge compared to Grand Prairie's two rooms of books separated by an island of bound magazines. I often brought home a half a dozen books and promised to keep up with them so we could return them the next week. Those excursions were my favorite four hours of the week, about the same duration as the bus tour, come to think of it—unless *Robin Hood* happened to be showing on a school night. While other fathers were teaching their kids about hunting and camping or bike riding or home repairs, Fath, with his Chesterfield in his right hand and his boys in semitow, was turning us into bookstore and café boulevardiers. In his heart of hearts, he was a New Yorker in exile. I guess I became one, too. At Kepler's and then at Garner and Smith on the Drag and Book People on Sixth Street in Austin, I built upon what he taught me. Over the years—and with the help of Norma, who loves books even more than I do—I have been refining my technique and always seem to end up in one independent bookstore or another when traveling.

In Howard Street Booksellers, I continued my conversation with my fellow pilgrims Debra and her Target marketing colleague Nancy Berget. They were checking out Mary and Joe's Dylan books when I put in my unsolicited two cents, as I frequently overzealously do. "*The Rough Guide* is good general information, and Michael Gray's encyclopedia is essential for aspiring obsessives," I told them, sounding like a bit more of a know-it-all than I intended. "Oh, and you should probably get Yaffe's *Like a Complete Unknown*," I continued.

Nancy bought *The Rough Guide* and told me, back at Zimmy's, about being near Dylan's farm in Andover at one point a few years earlier. She, Debra, and I kept returning to something we had experienced at Echo's house, like Dylan kept returning to that Gregory Peck movie in "Brownsville Girl." Because of the tour, we felt as if we truly appreciated Engel's sentence about Echo and Bob: "He's Howard Street business and she's poor folks from the wrong side of Highway 169."[25] Echo and Bob's movie kept rolling through our heads and we had fun making it up. Of course, we were drawing from our own personal movies as we did so.

Then it was time for the second night of the Singer/Songwriter Contest. Gary was back at the mike, and the Duluth crew—Kathleen, John, Bill, Don, and Zane—was in for the event. Zane had taken the judicial baton from Caryn. Caryn and one of Zimmy's staff paid homage to Dylan by wearing leopard-skin pillbox hats. Wiley, who had been on the bus tour, was back at his filming station. Hoser was there. But not Carlos, who had headed west. I sat with Don, making notes on the participants from Iowa, Indiana, Wisconsin, and Minnesota. The same two Norwegian bachelor farmers, as I had taken to thinking of them in tribute to Minnesotan Garrison Keillor, sat at the same two stools at the end of the bar, under a photo of Dylan, Springsteen, and Sinatra together at Frank's birthday party. Winners of each evening's contest won a copy of the picture as well as some cash.

Don was great company, remarking that "attitude and edge matter" after Jarret Thompson performed "Jokerman." When another performer's introductory remarks went on too long, Don described him as "going on like he's a member of the '72 Steelers." We laughed, avoided talking about Franco Harris's "immaculate reception," and had another beer. I asked Don about his first interest in Dylan, and he told me that it was by way of the Byrds' "Mr. Tambourine Man," which he described as "a torrent of arcane words and images that did something better than tell the truth straight." (I made a note in my Moleskine to give Carlos double credit on his McGuinn thesis.) Then Don, who modestly described himself as "having some artistic tendencies," expanded upon what he heard in the music. For him, Dylan's lyrics "spoke to the truth, and began a process in my mind that led, years later, to the realization that myths and legends do the same thing. History is always seen in the light of subsequent events, but myths maintain their integrity over time and become imbedded in entire cultures."[26] He added that he particularly admired Dylan's "pugnacity." Don grew up on the Range, as people in Minnesota call the once iron-rich northeastern portion of their state, and observed, "I think most of his pugnacity was learned on the Range ... that's how people talk and treat each other, how they think and feel. Rangers are kind of born with a chip on their shoulders. But you have to believe in yourself to carry that off."[27]

Duluth electrician Jerry Schlafer offered a very understated "Rainy Day Women #12 & 35," during which much of the crowed chimed in on *everybody must get stoned.* Sheila Wonders rapped through "Subterranean Homesick Blues" and drummed softly on her guitar between verses, which made many people smile. Peter Kaye's "Isis" inspired a lively, right-on-time *well, I guess* from Don and me in response to *She said, 'You look different.'* When Chris Haise, who had been convinced by our emcee to play another night, won the evening's first prize, the roof barely stayed on. I high-fived Hoser and Wiley and Don—like we were some kind of latter-day '72 Steelers. Somebody said, "There is justice in the world." Chris's encore was a joyful "From a Buick 6," and we could barely hear the last stanza for all the cheering. Chris's girlfriend was glowing, and Hoser nodded my way.

The Adjustments, with a masking-tape "Adjust" on their drum set, then played three hours of all kinds of dance music from the Sixties and Seventies. Their "Sgt. Pepper's Lonely Hearts Club Band" was a particular crowd-pleaser. We regulars were joined on the floor by a couple of sisters and their (I assumed but never asked) husbands. Marilyn came in from the smoking porch and danced, like a latter-day Jennifer Grey in *Dirty Dancing*. She had that twenty-three-year-old energy that none of us had anymore. In fact, my guess is that only a few of us even remembered ever having it. Like her contemporaries on the train a few nights before, she knew every word to every song.

Pagel and Bushey were at a table discussing, I imagined, matters that I probably should have tried to get in on. But it wasn't my style to cross that line and go where I was not invited. Styble did ask me to talk with him about my "project." We talked about the bus tour and shared our mixed emotions about Christopher

Ricks's readings of Dylan's work. There was, no doubt, much I could have learned had I spent more time with Styble. He knew so much and had so many thoughts, and our conversation could have easily pivoted from five minutes into a few hours. But on my last night in Hibbing I just wanted to let the mysteries—the exact dates and the piano color—be.

After all, the Adjustments were covering Creedence and there were women in leopard-skin pillbox hats dancing. I thought about talking more with Styble or joining Pagel and Bushey. After about ten seconds, I decided to double down on my instincts. I went back out there and danced the rest of the night with my fellow, as Mr. Fox put it, "wild animals." We were the Fauves in the house.

When the Adjustments finished, I asked their teenage guitarist where they learned "all that great material." He replied, "From life, sir." Hoser, a taciturn character *most of the time*, gave me a going-away present when he told me what he thought Dylan's fans were about. "Dude," he said in response to the fan question I had been saving for the past twenty four hours, "Dylan fans share a religion. There are Protestant Dylan fans, Catholic Dylan fans, Jewish Dylan fans, agnostic Dylan fans. And when he's dead they're still gonna be there."[28] I couldn't write fast enough in my Moleskine, which had been returned to me by a kind stranger who found it on the floor in the other room. Hibbing is, indeed, a good ol' town. I told Kathleen and Bushey good-bye and good luck. We made noises about perhaps someday connecting in Austin, and he told me to let him know if he could help me out. I told him I'd catch up with him on the radio.

I wrote in the guest book on my way out. "Thanks for your intelligent hearts and bringing so many good people together under Dylan's tent." I thought about Natalie Goldberg's closing words in *Tangled Up in Bob*. She said, "You're not going to find Bob Dylan in Hibbing. You are maybe going to find yourself or something that you want."[29] I didn't really like that much when I first heard it. It was, however, starting to make sense to me. In fact, I got out of there pretty quick for fear that if I didn't, I might tip my emotional hand and go misty on them all.

My car was still by the dumpster, the dog was barking, and the police were out. They let me be. Cronenberg's *The Fly* was playing on my hotel room television. It was easy to turn off because Jeff Goldblum was already starting to spin around on that exercise bar at an eerie speed. After less than five minutes of thinking about turquoise, gold, and the world's biggest necklace, I fell into what Dylan might have called *a series of dreams*.

Sunday morning I arrived early for the Farewell Brunch and felt like Bill Murray's Phil Connor sitting outside the local bank in *Groundhog Day*. As I listened to Seamus Heaney reading his poem "The Otter" on KUMD's "Celtic Connections," Pierrette again walked through the alley with her morning cigarette, the armored truck guys pulled up at Wells Fargo right on time, there was the gust of wind, and the dog barked.

I went inside, greeted Mandy, and sat with Gary, Mary, Joe, and a couple more people. Although I had to get down the road before I could hear the local Ojibwe blessing, I ate a great breakfast and had two damn fine cups of coffee. Linda was completely voiceless. Bob H. helped me out, yet again, by finding a tube for my latest Dylan posters. We shared a few quick stories about our fathers, some movie quotes, and a good hug. Judge Caryn encouraged me to stop at Tobie's on my way to Minneapolis for what turned out to be a world-class cinnamon roll.

Characteristically early for my flight, I celebrated the completion of my mission with a Goose Island draft at Granddaddy's. I was so living the dream that I didn't even have to ask bartender Mitch Giblin to put the golf tournament on the big screen. Forty-three-year-old Jay Windsor, a futures trader on his way back to Chicago with his wife, Reyna, and their two young daughters, had already requested golf. Mitch, great airport bartender that he is, was making it happen. Lox for breakfast, a cinnamon roll at Tobie's, the back nine on Sunday at the airport on my way home. How much better could it get?

Amazingly, it got even better a few minutes later. As we watched golfer Boo Weekley hold on at Colonial and slip on the winner's plaid jacket, what should come on the sound system but "Like a Rolling Stone"? Jay, whom I had told that I came in for Dylan Days, said, as if I had written it for him, "What an attitude he had at twenty-five! He was like a Shelley or a Keats." Mitch agreed and added, "All that music over all these years!" I thought about my favorite quotation from someone other than Bob Dylan or Fath: Catherine of Siena's "All the way to heaven is heaven."[30]

As my seventy-two hours in Minnesota—starting with the kid at the Enterprise desk and ending with my fellow music historians at Granddaddy's—came to an end, I also thought of the words of Debby Ellis, who used to observe about one wonder after another—from the news of the world to the academic shenanigans of our colleagues—"You can't make this shit up." No kidding, Debby, I thought as I finished my Goose Island.

As fate would have it, that "Like a Rolling Stone" moment with my fellow fans was not the end of this particular chapter in my Dylan story. As I settled into the back row on my flight home, it didn't take me very long to tell my neighbors that I had been in for Dylan Days. David Skinner, a junior theology major in Minneapolis on his way to Vermont, asked me, "Why should I like someone with such a bad voice?"

When the other person in our row, a retired high school teacher, chimed in, "He's dead now, but was pretty good when he did 'Country Roads,'" I knew I wasn't in Zimmy's or even Granddaddy's anymore.

I chose not to correct her and started off with my "Dylan has many voices" spiel. Young Skinner was attentive, but looked unconvinced. Jay was in the seat in front of me, putting on his headphones and probably aware that I was swimming upstream. The retiree mentioned "Country Roads" again. I breathed through my eyelids, counted to five, and tried to refrain from the Pee-wee Herman-in-the-Alamo eye roll that Norma tells me I do too often in my moments of frustration and impatience.

I hope that I was polite when, on the count of six, I slowly stated, "I think you're talking about John Denver."

"Oh yeah," she said. "You're right. Tell me about Bob ... is it Dylan?"

I gave her the broad strokes, and an occasional key detail, most of the way to Chicago. After all, I am a teacher and was returning from Hibbing more determined than ever to have *nothing but affection for those who have sailed with me*. Maybe I even started Young Skinner and the Retiree on their ways to becoming Dylan fans. Stranger things have happened. I bid them fare thee well and lucked into an empty row on the flight to Austin. I put on my headphones and hit shuffle. I don't really remember what song played first.

AFTERWORD

I did not return to Dylan Days the following May. Instead, I worked on my manuscript, attended two conferences related to student scholarships, and prepared for my fall classes. I rationalized that there was no way XIV could top XIII. Dylan Days—with the Blood on the Tracks Express and the Writer's Contest and an exhibition of Donald Kramer's photographs and a visit from Dave Kinney, who had just published *The Dylanologists*—did somehow go on without me.

There were reasons I was alright with missing it. Zimmy's had closed, hopefully temporarily, due to some financial difficulties. Bookstore Mary and I talked on the phone, and she told me that she wasn't sure that, after "a particularly rough winter," Howard Street Booksellers would be able to make it another year. Brother Phil Fitzpatrick won second place in the fiction category for his short story "Foul Shot," but wrote me that he was not going to be there this year due to a family graduation in Boulder. Carlos had written a story titled "Car Trouble in Carver County," but I had temporarily lost touch with him as well as Hoser Engel. It seemed pretty clear that neither Bob nor, as once rumored, Jakob Dylan would be making a surprise appearance. I told myself that the universe wanted me elsewhere.

So I met and planned and wrote and revised, believing that the right way to end *In Dylan Town* would, like so many of the best things in my life, come to me at the right time. Then, in an airplane on the way to Des Moines, I read the following words from Carol Ann Fitzgerald in the anthology I had ordered for my first-year seminar: "When it comes to music, we project what we most crave onto its makers. When we listen to certain tunes—and play them for our friends—we are making a statement of who we are or who we want to be."[1] Imagine my delight. Fitzgerald had given me my ending.

Through no conscious decision on my part, the word *crave* had not appeared anywhere in *In Dylan Town*. It is not a word I have ever used very much. However, so much of what I associate with the word runs through these pages. My cravings—from when I first started watching movies, hearing music, and longing for the perfect love to this very moment when I keep wanting to be a better teacher and to have more time with my family and friends and music—have defined, simultaneously, who I am and who I want to be.

It makes sense that I and so many of the people I have loved, my fellow fans and students among them, are works-in-progress who, as Fitzgerald put it, "project" our cravings on to the greatest work-in-progress of our time. After all, it was he who told us years ago and frequently reminds us, *he not busy being born is busy dying.*

Listening to 1975 Rolling Thunder Dylan a few nights ago in the gloaming, Norma and I heard a cha-cha version of "Tonight I'll Be Staying Here with You" slide into the theatricality of "Isis" and give way to the acoustic beauty of "Mr. Tambourine Man" before closing the twenty-two-song set list with a transcendent "Knockin' on Heaven's Door." We were in tears.

Needing reassurance yet again, I asked Norma, "Is he really as amazing as I think he is? Who has ever done what he has done?"

She waited a few beats and then, latecomer to Dylan fandom that she is, said, "No one. He does with words what Gershwin did with notes. And he's a rogue to boot."

I liked that we agreed, even if the Gershwin reference was beyond me, and I loved the word *rogue.* It's a fine word that's well suited to Bob—and to all of my other heroes, for that matter. As we talked, I realized that over the course of my project I had grown even more swept away by Dylan's art.

The very next day I was talking about Dylan and life with Virginia Carwell, the English Department chair who hired me for the job I found posted above the Parlin Hall Dr. Pepper machine all those years ago. She had recently read an article about literary biographers losing respect for their subjects the deeper they immersed themselves in them and was particularly taken with a writer who stated, "The more time you spend with Chekhov the more you have to respect him." I saw her question coming: "After all your work, how do you feel about Dylan?"[2]

I thought about how I really felt and searched for the best way to put it. The closest I could come was "I love his stuff more than ever." Then like the Dylan fan I am, I added, "As he put it in 'You Angel You,' *If this is love then gimme more / And more and more and more.*"

That worked for Virginia, who smiled and said, "Very good." Then we moved on to talking about what I would be teaching in the fall.

Georgetown, Texas

ACKNOWLEDGMENTS

It took a few villages to bring *In Dylan Town* all the way home. It is almost as daunting a task to acknowledge those who have sailed with me as it was to write the book. What follows is my best effort to reconstruct all my guides, spirits, and coconspirators along the way. I apologize in advance to anyone who I inadvertently fail to mention. To all, mentioned and otherwise, I am more thankful than I can possibly express. You also bear no responsibility for any erroneous or lame moments in the book. Those are all of my own making, in spite of your best advice and examples.

The crew at the University of Iowa Press—Karen, James, Allison, Faye, Elisabeth, Amy, and Susan—managed to make sense of my manuscript and make it look even better before it came into the world. Their holiday card each year made me feel part of the family, a family I did not want to disappoint. Clare Jones read my embarrassing first draft and offered invaluable advice for the next one. Valerie Ahwee and Susan Hill Newton not only put up with but also improved upon the changes I continued making way beyond the time that *the hour [was] getting late*. Catherine Cocks, the acquisitions editor with whom this all began, also read that first draft, gave me the chance to write a second draft, and got the train on the right track. In her next acts of alchemy, she made subsequent drafts even better. She was my dream-come-true editor—incredibly smart, very prompt, remarkably patient, and willing to laugh—every step of the way. She is *the brains behind Pa*.

Terry Sherrell and another crew—the gang at OneTouchPoint in Austin—got my manuscript in shape for submission on short notice. They, like the good people in Iowa City, helped me on some of the permissions that so many people generously granted me. They did all of this in spite of the fact that Crosby, Stills, and Nash came to town right around our deadline. It was fun to turn it all over to them and even more fun to see what they produced. Callie Gladman at Special Rider Music also deserves a major shout-out for her generous and efficient help with the Dylan permissions. She spared me many strange dreams. Murray Lerner, whose amazing documentary *Festival!* provided many of the key images in my head, generously allowed me to use one of those images and shared a magical half hour on the phone with me as I was completing this project. Kris Luck provided the jacket photograph of me and made me look far better than I do in real life.

My Dylan friends, both at conferences and various publications, gave me room to play and shaped my thinking about my long-running attachment to Dylan's art and life. Primary among them has been Nina Goss, editor of *Montague Street* and *Dylan at Play*. If I could think and write anywhere near as clearly or elegantly as Nina, this would be an even better book. Nick Smart, Nina's coeditor of *Dylan at Play*, helped make sense of my article about Dylan and transnationalism. I presented the paper that turned into that chapter of *Dylan at Play* at the New England Modern Language Association meeting on a panel organized by Adam Lifshey of Georgetown University. It was there that Nina, Nick, and I became partners in victimless crime. Bob Levinson of the New School invited me to talk about Dylan when I was just starting to do so beyond my classroom. When Nina inherited the class from Levinson, she generously kept that ball rolling. Schreiner University's Kathleen Hudson, founder of the Texas Heritage Music Foundation, connected me with the Young Rhetoricians Conference in Monterey, California, where I spoke and received very helpful responses from a roomful of deeply committed teachers. Frances Hunter, a fellow Dylanist at Arkansas State University, oversaw a labor of love titled *Professing Dylan* and, in the spring of 2015, brought a lot of Dylan fans and teachers together at the Delta Blues Symposium for a magical day. The people at the Experience Music Project Pop Conference in Seattle (particularly Eric Weisbard and John Shaw) were supportive colleagues. So were my fellow panelists regarding humor (in San Antonio in 2011) and fandom (in Boston in 2012) at the annual meetings of the Popular Culture and American Culture Associations and the participants at the annual meetings of the American Studies Association of Texas. My sense of Dylan and his place with both his fans and our students has been greatly enriched by all of those good conversations in and out of print.

As Chapter Four points out, I met several terrific fellow fans in Duluth and Hibbing when I attended Dylan Days. In alphabetical order they are Zane Bail, Aaron Brown, Don Dass, Dave Engel, Phil Fitzpatrick, Babe Glumack, Bob Hocking, C. E. "Carlos" Holmes, Jamie Kallestad, Mary and Joe Keyes, Tony Petersen, Linda Stroback, and Caryn Wilder. Several of them have generously permitted me to quote from our correspondence. I look forward to future Dylan Days with them and our correspondences across all the miles in between.

I have also had plenty of Dylan friends among my colleagues and students over the course of my thirty years at Southwestern University. Southwestern has supported my research and teaching as well as my participation in conferences. For that and so much more I am deeply thankful. The A. Frank Smith, Jr. Library—and particularly Lisa Anderson in Interlibrary Loan, Mary Fields in Periodicals, and Carol Fonken in Research and Digital Scholarship—have kept me in the loop and many times shown me a new dimension of it. The library's Writer's Voice Program, which Lynne Brody choreographed, provided me and the rest of the campus community opportunities to spend time with writers whom I could only hope to grow up to be more like. Chief among them were Russell Banks, T. C. Boyle, Michael Chabon, Dave Eggers, and Tony Kushner. Provost Jim Hunt and presidents Jake Schrum and Edward Burger encouraged me to follow my muses and supported my work in every possible way. My tech wiz colleagues Eric Bumgardner and Andrew Rechnitz did magical work on preparing images for all my Dylan-related projects and have taught me much and shared some laughs along the way. My conversations in the hallways, through e-mail, and at meals with Virginia Carwell, Daniel Castro, Eileen Cleere, Sergio Costola, Julie Cowley, Dirk Early, Debby Ellis, Fumiko Futamura, Dan Hilliard, Thomas Howe, Jim Kilfoyle, John McCann, Elisabeth Piedmont-Marton, John Pipkin, Jesse Purdy, Eric Selbin, Patrick Veerkamp, and Dan Yoxall made me a clearer thinker and this a better book than it would have been without the gift of their friendships. They join Gail Caldwell, Bill deBuys, Dana Joseph, Michael McCarry, Mike Mooneyham, Jim Neff, Bob Payne, David Stansbury, John Taliaferro, and Jerome Weeks as fellow travelers and kindred spirits from various classrooms, editorial offices, and past lives.

My companions at numerous tables of joy are no doubt breathing a collective sigh of relief to see *In Dylan Town* finally come to fruition. They have listened to me talk about it for years and have been incredibly patient and supportive. We have burned some evening oil, lifted a few glasses, and had some adventures. I look forward to more of the same and new conversations about my next project with David Aguirre, Vincent Aguirre, Paul Aguirre and Amy Stephenson, Lisa and Richard Anderson, Diane and Jim Hunt, Ed Kain, Polly Gorin and Bob Payne, and Mary and Patrick Veerkamp. I promise it will not take quite as long as this one did and that I will try not only to get to the point sooner but also to listen better.

I hope that every page of this book underscores the importance of teachers and students in my life. After all, I continue to be both. Everyone I have acknowledged so far has taught me, as did my most important official teachers—Bliss Carnochan, Bill Chace, Bill Goetzmann, Kay Powell, Walter Sokel,

Bill Stephenson, Bill Stott, Wick Wadlington, Jim Wallis, T. B. L. Webster, and Bob Weston. They all made me want to be a teacher. I have had the great fortune to work with hundreds of students who have kept me honest and made me smarter. What they saw and heard in Dylan's work, and in my non-Dylan classes as well, continued to convince me that I was on to something. Just because it's a cliché doesn't mean it's not true: they taught me far more than I ever taught them. My best teachers in that rogues' gallery are my friends Lindsey Albracht, Deanne Armstrong, Mitch Barnett, Mary Luisa Berges, Christopher Chaput, Sadie Clarendon, Alison Dickson, Delilah Dominguez, Casey Douglas, Meagan Elliott, Robert Faires, Dori Glanz, Kimberly Lacy, and Joseph Strickland. They are keepin' on and making the world a better place.

Above all, I want to acknowledge what I continue to believe *it's all about*—my family. It is to them that *In Dylan Town* is dedicated. When I write *family* I am thinking of my parents, my blood brother, Steve, and our sister, Melissa. I am also thinking of the Alanizes and the Aguirres, the two families I married into, and the parents and brothers and sisters with which so doing has blessed me. Most of all, though, I want to acknowledge and thank Buddy, Kell, Rach, and Sid, who are far and away my favorite band of wild animals and the providers of ineffable joy. Then there is Norma, with whom this yarn began. She is still my best editor, traveling companion, and truest north after all these years. She and the kids are my reason for it all.

NOTES

PREFACE

1. Jacobson, "Tangled Up in Bob" 74.
2. Edmundson, *Why Read?* 121.
3. Ellen, "Useless and Pointless Knowledge" 515.
4. Edmundson 45.
5. Stott, *Write to the Point* 114.
6. Shields, *Reality Hunger* 101.
7. Didion, *Slouching Towards Bethlehem* 41.
8. Lethem, *"Fear of Music"* 406.

CHAPTER ONE

1. Heylin, *Bob Dylan: A Life in Stolen Moments* 7.
2. Gray, *The Bob Dylan Encyclopedia*.
3. Gray, *Song and Dance Man III* 5.
4. Jaffe, "808 Cities."
5. Dettmar, *The Cambridge Companion*.
6. Dettmar 1.
7. *Telegraph* Apr. 5, 2014.
8. Crouch, *Dylan TV*.
9. Jacobson 72.
10. Duffett, *Understanding Fandom*.
11. Duffett 293.
12. Jenkins, *Textual Poachers* 2.
13. Jenkins 45.
14. Jenkins 36.
15. Gray, *Encyclopedia* 524.
16. Gray, *Encyclopedia* 12–13.
17. Gray, *Encyclopedia* 38.
18. Barker, ed., *Isis* x.
19. Barker 13.
20. Barker 13.
21. Johnson, *Encounters with Bob Dylan*.
22. Johnson ix.
23. Atton, "Fanzines" 226.

24. Atton 227.

25. Strachan, "Where Do I Begin" 76–77.

26. Coviello, "The Talk" 11.

27. Gopnik, "The In-Law" 57.

28. P. Williams, "Bob Dylan" 18.

29. P. Williams 17.

30. P. Williams 9.

31. P. Williams 10.

32. Gray, *Encyclopedia* 707.

33. Gray, *Encyclopedia* 39.

34. Cott, *Dylan*.

35. Cott iv.

36. Gray, *Encyclopedia* 40.

37. Bauldie, "All About *The Telegraph*,"
    http:/expectingrain.com/div/telegraph/info

38. Gray, *Encyclopedia* 693.

39. Gray, *Encyclopedia*.

40. Bauldie.

41. Barker 321.

42. Shepard, *Rolling Thunder Logbook*.

43. Shepard 89.

44. R. Williams, *Dylan* 11.

45. Shields and Salerno.

46. Bauldie.

47. Kelly, "Fans, Collectors" 249.

48. Kelly 250.

49. Kelly 252.

50. Kelly 252.

51. Proverbs 18:15.

52. Carpenter, "Bob Dylan and the New Humanities" 64.

53. Johnson, *Encounters*.

54. Johnson 52.

55. Johnson xii.

56. Johnson viii.

57. Johnson 39.

58. Johnson viii, 40, 164, 167.

59. Des Barres.

60. Johnson 55.

61. Johnson 54.

62. Sloman, *On the Road*.

63. Sloman 74.

64. Sloman 212–13.

65. Sloman 460–61.

66. Jenkins 251.

67. Johnson 45.

68. Jenkins 251.

69. Johnson 167.

70. Johnson 173.

71. Johnson 173.

72. B. Williams, My Bob Dylan Story.

73. B. Williams.

74. B. Williams.

75. B. Williams.

76. Shenk and Silberman; Doss; Cavicchi.

77. Duffett, to David Gaines, May 16, 2012. E-mail.

78. Duffett.

79. Weiner.

80. Weiner 36.

81. Weiner 151.

82. Chabon, "Dylan at Sixty" 256.

83. Chabon 256.

84. Chabon, "Let It Rock" 28.

85. Gray *Encyclopedia* 274.

86. Gray *Encyclopedia* 275.

87. Gray, *Song* 420.

88. Gray, *Song* 212.

89. Gray, *Encyclopedia* 274.

90. Gegenbuber.

91. Gegenbuber.

92. Gray, *Encyclopedia* 311.

93. Gray, *Encyclopedia* 311.

94. Heylin, *Bob Dylan: The Recording Sessions* xi.

95. Heylin, *Recording Sessions* 504.

96. Gray, *Encyclopedia* 311.

97. Willis, *Out of the Vinyl Deeps* 77.

98. Willis 77.

99. Willis 9.

100. Willis 207.

101. Willis 147.

102. Willis 215.

103. Ross, *Listen to This* 286–87.

104. Curnyn.

105. Gray, *Encyclopedia* 645.

106. Styble, *Radioactive Dylan*.

107. Gray, *Encyclopedia* 196.

108. Gray, *Encyclopedia* 196.

109. P. Williams 134.

110. P. Williams 64.

111. P. Williams 65.

112. P. Williams 100.

113. P. Williams 131–32.

114. P. Williams 133.

115. *Montague Street* 2.

116. Shepard 73.

117. Gray, *Encylopedia* 451.

118. Marcus, *The Old Weird America*.

119. Marcus, *Like a Rolling Stone*.

120. Marcus, *Bob Dylan by Greil Marcus* xvi.

121. Marcus, *Greil Marcus* xvii.

122. Marcus, ed., *Stranded*.

123. Marcus, *Stranded* 267.

124. Marcus, *Greil Marcus* 7.

125. Marcus, *Greil Marcus* 23.

126. Marcus, *Greil Marcus* 24.

127. Marcus, "Another Self Portrait."

128. Marcus, "Another Self Portrait" 34.

129. Marcus, "Another Self Portrait" 34.

130. Gray, *Encyclopedia* 451.

131. Sante, "I Is Someone Else" 39.

132. Sante 39.

133. Emerson, "Nature" 371.

CHAPTER TWO

1. Lévi-Strauss, *Tristes Tropiques* (1955 ed.).

2. Lévi-Strauss, 19.

3. Ellison, *Invisible Man* 3.

4. Ellison 581.

5. Dylan, *Chronicles* 51.

6. Kael, *The Age of Movies*.

7. Melville, *Moby-Dick* 435.

8. Melville 234.

9. Coviello 10.

10. Coviello 11.

CHAPTER THREE

1. Salinger, *The Catcher in the Rye* 1.

2. White, "The Second Tree" 127.

3. Lennon and Ono 132.

4. Ellison 33.

5. J. Heller, *Catch-22* 15.

6. Shaw.

7. Gilmore, "Bob Dylan at Fifty" 60.

8. Hass, *Praise* 5.

9. Salinger 213.

CHAPTER FOUR

1. Kallestad, e-mail to David Gaines, June 12, 2013.

2. Kallestad.

3. Kallestad.

4. Kallestad.

5. Petersen, e-mail to David Gaines, June 10, 2013.

6. Marcus, *Like a Rolling Stone* 65.

7. Marcus, "Hibbing High School" 5.

8. Dylan, "My Life in a Stolen Moment" 5.

9. Fitzpatrick, letter to David Gaines, June 10, 2013.

10. Fitzpatrick.

11. Wilder, letter to David Gaines, July 27, 2013.

12. Brown, *Overburden* 208.

13. Brown 210.

14. Brown 216.

15. Gray, *Encyclopedia* 209–10.

16. Glumack, letter to David Gaines, June 18, 2013.

17. Holmes, letter to David Gaines, June 18, 2013.

18. Holmes.
19. Kitchen 11.
20. N. Heller, "Laptop U" 83.
21. Marcus, "Hibbing High School" 12.
22. Feidt 12.
23. Hoikkala.
24. Scobie, *Alias Bob Dylan* 66.
25. Engel, *Just Like Bob Zimmerman's Blues* 175.
26. Dass, letter to David Gaines, June 14 2013.
27. Dass.
28. Engel, *Just Like Bob Zimmerman's Blues*.
29. Feidt.
30. Matthiessen, *The Snow Leopard* 58.

AFTERWORD

1. Fitzgerald, *Bessie Smith* 20.
2. Carwell.

WORKS CITED

Alterman, Eric. "Presleyites, Dylanists, and Springsteenians." *The New York Times Book Review* Jan. 30, 2000. 27. Print.

Andersen, Karl Erik. *Expecting Rain.* Web. http://expectingrain.com. August 1, 2013.

Anderson, Donald. *Gathering Noise from My Life: A Camouflaged Memoir.* Iowa City: U of Iowa P, 2012. Print.

Atton, Chris. "Fanzines." *Continuum Encyclopedia of Popular Music of the World.* Vol. I: *Media, Industry, and Society.* Ed. John Sheperd, David Horn, Dave Laing, Paul Oliver, and Peter Wicke. London: Continuum International, 2003. 226–28. Print.

Barker, Derek. *Bob Dylan Anthology.* Vol. 2: *20 Years of Isis.* Surrey UK: Chrome Dreams, 2005. Print.

———, ed. *Isis: A Bob Dylan Anthology.* London: Helter Skelter, 2001. Print.

Bauldie, John. "All About *The Telegraph.*" Web. http:/expectingrain.com/div/telegraph/info. July 15, 2013.

———, ed. *Wanted Man: In Search of Bob Dylan.* New York: Citadel, 1990. Print.

Bobdylan.com. Web. http://www.bobdylan.com. July 1, 2013.

Brown, Aaron. *Overburden: Modern Life on the Iron Range.* Duluth: Red Step, 2008. Print.

Carpenter, William. "Bob Dylan and the New Humanities." *Montague Street* 2 (2010): 62–65. Print.

Carwell, Virginia A. Interview by David Gaines. August 1, 2014.

Cavicchi, Daniel. *Tramps Like Us: Music and Meaning among Springsteen Fans.* New York: Oxford UP, 1998. Print.

Chabon, Michael. "Dylan at Sixty." *Studio A: The Bob Dylan Reader.* Ed. Benjamin Hedin. New York: W. W. Norton and Company, 2004. 255–57. Print.

———. "Foreword." *Trickster Makes This World: Mischief, Myth, and Art* by Lewis Hyde. New York: Farrar, Straus, and Giroux, 2010. xi–xii. Print.

———. "Let It Rock." *The New York Review of Books* July 11, 2013: 26–27.

Chiasson, Dan. "The 'Stoned Gallantry' of Leonard Cohen." *New York Review of Books* Feb. 21, 2013: 10–14. Print.

Corcoran, Neil, ed. *"Do You, Mr. Jones?": Bob Dylan with the Poets and Professors.* London: Chatto and Windus, 2002. Print.

Cott, Jonathan. *Dylan.* Garden City: Rolling Stone, 1984. Print.

Coviello, Peter. "The Talk That Does Not Do Nothing." *The Believer* 10.6: 7–11. Print.

Crouch, Ian. *Dylan TV.* Web. http://www.newyorker.com/online/blogs/culture2013/11/ bob-dylan, Nov. 20, 2013.

Curnyn, Sean. Web. http://www.rightwingbob.com. July 20, 2013.

Dass, Don. Letter to David Gaines. June 14, 2013. Typescript.

Des Barres, Pamela. *I'm with the Band: Confessions of a Groupie*. Chicago: Chicago River, 1987. Print.

Dettmar, Kevin J. H., ed. *The Cambridge Companion to Bob Dylan*. Cambridge: Cambridge UP, 2009. Print.

Didion, Joan. *Slouching Towards Bethlehem*. New York: Dell, 1968. Print.

Doss, Erika. *Elvis Culture: Fans, Faith & Image*. Lawrence: UP of Kansas. 1999. Print.

Dreamtime: Commentary Inspired by Bob Dylan's Theme Time Radio. Web. http://www. dreamtimepodcast.com. July 20, 2013.

Duffett, Mark. Message to David Gaines. May 16, 2012. E-mail.

———. *Understanding Fandom: An Introduction to the Study of Media Fan Culture*. New York: Bloomsbury, 2013. Print.

Dylan, Bob. *Chronicles*. Vol. 1. New York: Simon and Schuster, 2004. Print.

———. *The Drawn Blank Series*. New York: Prestel, 2008. Print.

———. *Lyrics 1962–2001*. New York: Simon and Schuster, 2004. Print.

———. "My Life in a Stolen Moment." *Studio A: The Bob Dylan Reader*. Ed. Benjamin Hedin. New York: W. W. Norton and Company, 2004. 3–7. Print.

———. *Tarantula*. New York: Macmillan Company, 1966. Print.

Eco, Umberto. *Travels in Hyper Reality: Essays*. San Diego: Harcourt Brace Jovanovich, 1986. Print.

Edmundson, Mark. *Why Read?* New York: Bloomsbury, 2004. Print.

———. *Why Teach?* New York: Bloomsbury, 2013. Print.

Egan, Seth. *The Mammoth Book of Bob Dylan*. London: Running, 2011. Print.

Ellen, Mark. "Useless and Pointless Knowledge." *The Mammoth Book of Bob Dylan*. Ed. Sean Egan. Philadelphia: Running, 2011. 513–16. First published as "Memory Almost Full" in *The Word*, April 2009. Print.

Ellison, Ralph. *Invisible Man*. New York: Random House, 1989. Print.

Emerson, Ralph Waldo. "Nature." *Ralph Waldo Emerson: An Organic Anthology*. Ed. Stephen E. Whicher. Boston: Houghton Mifflin, 1957. 21–56. Print.

Engel, Dave. Interview by David Gaines. May 25, 2013.

———. *Just Like Bob Zimmerman's Blues: Dylan in Minnesota*. Rudolph: River City Memoirs-Mesabi, 1997. Print.

Fitzgerald, Carol Ann. "Bessie Smith: Any Woman's Blues." *The Oxford American Book of Great Music Writing*. Ed. Marc Smirnoff. Fayetteville: U of Arkansas P, 2008. 14–24. Print.

Fitzpatrick, Phil. Letter to David Gaines. June 10, 2013. Typescript.

Frere-Jones, Sasha. "Foreword: Opening the Vault." *Out of the Vinyl Deeps: Ellen Willis on Rock Music* by Ellen Willis. Minneapolis: U of Minnesota P, 2011. ix–xiv. Print.

Fricke, David. "Remembering Paul Williams, the First Rock Critic." Web. http.// www. Rollingstone.com/music/blogs/alternate-take/remembering-paul-williams-the-first- rock-critic-20130402. August 3, 2013.

Gadfly: Culture That Matters. Web. http://www.gadflyonline.com. July 28, 2013.

Gardening with Bob Dylan. Web. http://gardenleafing.blogsopt.com. July 15, 2013.

Geertz, Clifford. *The Interpretation of Cultures.* New York: Basic Books, 2000. Print.

———. *Works and Lives: The Anthropologist as Author.* Stanford: Stanford UP, 1988. Print.

Gegenhuber, Kurt. *The Celestial Monochord.* Web. http://celestialmonochord.org. July 24, 2013.

Gilmore, Mikal. "Bob Dylan at Fifty." *Rolling Stone* May 30, 1991: 56–60. Print.

Ginsberg, Allen. "On Reading Dylan's Writings." *Studio A: The Bob Dylan Reader.* Ed. Benjamin Hedin. New York: W. W. Norton and Company, 2004. 92–93. Print.

Glumack, Babe. Letter to David Gaines. June 18, 2013. Manuscript.

Gopnik, Adam. "The In-Law." *The New Yorker* Oct. 7, 2002: 56–61. Print.

Goss, Nina. *Gardener Is Gone.* Web. http://gardenerisgone.com. June 17, 2013.

Gray, Jonathan, Cornel Sandvoss, and C. Lee Harrington. *Fandom: Identities and Communities in a Mediated World.* New York: New York UP, 2007. Print.

Gray, Michael. *The Bob Dylan Encyclopedia.* New York: Continuum International, 2006. Print.

———. *Bob Dylan Encyclopedia: A Blog, 2006–2012.* Web. http:// bobdylanencyclopedia. blogspot.com. July 1, 2013.

———. *Song and Dance Man III.* London: Cassell, 2000. Print.

Gray, Michael, and John Bauldie, eds. *All Across the Telegraph: A Bob Dylan Handbook.* London: Sidgwick & Jackson, 1987. Print.

Guins, Raiford, and Omayra Zaragoza Cruz, eds. *Popular Culture: A Reader.* London: Sage, 2005. Print.

Hass, Robert. *Praise.* New York: Ecco, 1979. Print.

Hedin, Benjamin, ed. *Studio A: The Bob Dylan Reader.* New York: W. W. Norton and Company, 2004. Print.

Heller, Joseph. *Catch-22.* New York: Simon and Schuster, 1996. Print.

Heller, Nathan. "Laptop U." *New Yorker* May 20, 2013: 80–91. Print.

Heylin, Clinton. *Bob Dylan: A Life in Stolen Moments.* New York: Scribner Books, 1996. Print.

———. *Bob Dylan: The Recording Sessions 1960–1994.* New York: St. Martin's, 1995. Print.

———. *Bootleg: The Secret History of the Other Recording Industry.* New York: St.

Martin's Griffin, 1996. Print.

———. *Still on the Road: The Songs of Bob Dylan, 1974–2006*. Chicago: Chicago Review, 2010. Print.

Hills, Matt. *Fan Cultures*. London: Routledge, 2002. Print.

Hocking, Bob. Interview with David Gaines. May 24, 2013.

———. Interview with David Gaines. May 26, 2013.

Hoikkala, LeRoy. Interview with David Gaines. May 25, 2013.

Holmes, C. E. Letter to David Gaines. June 18, 2013. Typescript.

Hudson, Kathleen. *Telling Stories, Writing Songs: An Album of Texas Songwriters*. Austin: U of Texas P, 2001. Print.

———. *Women in Music: Stories and Songs*. Austin: U of Texas P, 2007. Print.

Hyde, Lewis. *Trickster Makes This World: Mischief, Myth, and Art*. New York: Farrar, Straus, and Giroux, 1998. Print.

Jacobson, Mark. "Tangled Up in Bob." *Rolling Stone* Apr. 21, 2001: 64–74, 151. Print.

Jaffe, Eric. "808 Cities, 2,503 Shows, and 1,007,416 Miles: The Staggering Geography of Bob Dylan's 'Never Ending Tour.'" *The Atlantic Cities* June 7, 2013. Print.

Jenkins, Henry. "Afterword: The Future of Fandom." *Fandom: Identities and Communities in a Mediated World*. Ed. Jonathan Gray, Cornel Sandvoss, and C. Lee Harrington. New York: New York UP, 2007. 357–64. Print.

———. *Textual Poachers*. London: Routledge, 1992. Print.

Johnson, Tracy. *Encounters with Bob Dylan: If You See Him Say Hello*. Daly City: Humble, 2000. Print.

Kael, Pauline. *The Age of Movies: Selected Writings of Pauline Kael*. Ed. Sanford Schartz. New York: Library of America, 2011. Print.

Kallestad, Jamie. Message to David Gaines. June 12, 2013. E-mail.

Kelly, Roy. "Fans, Collectors, and *Biograph*." *All Across the Telegraph: A Bob Dylan Handbook*. Ed. Michael Gray and John Bauldie. London: Sidgwick and Jackson, 1987. 243–53. Print.

Kinney, David. *The Dylanologists: Adventures in the Land of Bob*. New York: Simon and Schuster, 2014. Print.

Kitchen, Robert. *Hibbing, Minnesota: On the Move Since 1893*. Hibbing: Hibbing Public Library, 1991. Print.

Kristen, Susanne, and Stephen Dine Young. "A Foreign Sound to Your Ear: The Influence of Bob Dylan's Music on American and German-Speaking Fans." *Popular Music and Society* 32.2: 229–48. Print.

Lapham, Lewis. "The Solid Nonpareil." *Lapham's Quarterly* 7.1: 13–19. Print.

Leland, John. *Hip: The History*. New York: HarperCollins, 2004. Print.

Lennon, John, and Yoko Ono. *The Playboy Interviews with John Lennon and Yoko Ono.*

Ed. G. Barry Golson and conducted by David Sheff. New York: Playboy, 1981. Print.

Lepidus, Harold. *Bob Dylan Examiner*. Web. http://www.examiner.com/bob-dylan-in- national/Harold-lepidus. August 1, 2013.

Lethem, Jonathan. *Fear of Music*. New York: Continuum International, 2012. Print.

———. *The Fortress of Solitude*. New York: Random House, 2003. Print.

Lévi-Strauss, Claude. *Tristes Tropiques*. London: Penguin Books, 1955. Print.

Levi-Strauss, Claude. *Tristes Tropiques*. New York: Atheneum, 1974. Print.

Lewis, Lisa, ed. *The Adoring Audience: Fan Culture and Popular Media*. London: Routledge, 1992. Print.

Marcus, Greil. "Another Self Portrait." *The Bootleg Series*. Vol. 10: *Another Self Portrait*. New York: Columbia Records Division of Sony Music Corporation, 2013. Print.

———. *Bob Dylan by Greil Marcus: Writings 1968–2010*. New York: Public Affairs, 2010. Print.

———. "Hibbing High School and 'the Mystery of Democracy.'" *Highway 61 Revisited: Bob Dylan's Rod from Minnesota to the World*. Ed. Colleen J. Sheehy and Thomas Swiss. Minneapolis: U of Minnesota P, 2009. 3–14. Print.

———. *Like a Rolling Stone: Bob Dylan at the Crossroads*. New York: Public Affairs, 2005. Print.

———. *The Old, Weird America: The World of Bob Dylan's Basement Tapes*. New York: Picador, 1997. Print.

———, ed. *Stranded: Rock and Roll for a Desert Island*. New York: Alfred A. Knopf, Inc., 1979. Print.

Matthiessen, Peter. *The Snow Leopard*. New York: Viking, 1978. Print.

Melville, Herman. *Moby-Dick or, The Whale*. New York: Penguin Books, 1992. Print.

Montague Street: The Art of Bob Dylan 1(2009): 5–129. Print.

Moody, Rick. "*Blood on the Tracks*." *Studio A: The Bob Dylan Reader*. Ed. Benjamin Hedin. New York: W. W. Norton and Company, 2004. 109–12. Print.

O'Dair, Barbara. "Bob Dylan and Gender Politics." *The Cambridge Companion to Bob Dylan*. Ed. Kevin J. H. Dettmar. Cambridge: Cambridge UP, 2009. 80–86. Print.

Pagel, Bill. *Bob Links*. Web. http://www.boblinks.com. June 1, 2013.

Petersen, Tony. Message to David Gaines. June 10, 2013. E-mail.

Polito, Robert. "Shadow Play: B-C-D and Back." *Tin House* 3.2: 188–96. Print.

Polizzotti, Mark. *Highway 61 Revisited*. New York: Continuum International Publishing,2006. Print.

Ranson-Polizzotti, Sadi. *Tant Mieux*. Web. http://tantmieux.squarespace.com/bob-dylan- on-tant-mieux. June 15, 2013.

Ross, Alex. *Listen to This*. New York: Farrar, Straus, and Giroux, 2010. Print.

Salinger, J. D. *The Catcher in the Rye*. Boston: Little, Brown and Company, 1951. Print.

Sante, Luc. "I Is Someone Else." *New York Review of Books* Mar. 10, 2005. Print.

Scobie, Stephen. *Alias Bob Dylan, Revisited*. Calgary: Red Deer, 2003. Print.

———. *And Forget My Name: A Speculative Biography of Bob Dylan*. Victoria: Ekstasis Editions, 1999. Print.

Shaw, Kelley A. "Prophets" in Theology I at St. Michael's Catholic Academy. Dec. 3, 1999. Typescript.

Sheehy, Colleen J., and Thomas Swiss. *Highway 61 Revisited: Bob Dylan's Road from Minnesota to the World*. Minneapolis: U of Minnesota P, 2009. Print.

Shenk, David, and Steve Silberman. *Skeleton Key: A Dictionary for Deadheads*. New York: Doubleday, 1994. Print.

Shepard, Sam. *Rolling Thunder Logbook*. New York: Viking, 1977. Print.

Shields, David. *Reality Hunger: A Manifesto*. New York: Random House, 2010. Print.

Shields, David, and Shane Salerno. *Salinger*. New York: Simon and Schuster, 2013. Print.

Sloman, Larry. *On the Road with Bob Dylan*. New York: Three Rivers, 1978. Print.

Smart, Nick, and Nina Goss, eds. *Dylan at Play*. Newcastle upon Tyne: Cambridge Scholars, 2011. Print.

Smiley, Jane. "New Books." *Harper's Magazine* July 2013. Print.

Smith, Patti. *Just Kids*. New York: Ecco, 2010. Print.

Stott, Bill. *Write to the Point*. New York: Columbia UP, 1991. Print.

Strachan, Robert. "'Where Do I Begin the Story?': Collective Memory, Biographical Authority, and the Rock Biography." *Popular Music History* 3.1: 65–80. Print.

Styble, Bryan. *Radioactive Dylan*. Web. http://www.radioactivedylan.blogspot.com.

Tangled Up in Bob. Dir. Mary Feidt. Feido Films, 2011. Film.

Thompson, Toby. *Positively Main Street: Bob Dylan's Minnesota*. Minneapolis: U of Minnesota P, 2008. Print.

Vernezze, Peter, and Carl J. Porter, eds. *Bob Dylan and Philosophy*. Chicago: Open Court, 2006. Print.

Watts, Alan. *Tao: The Watercourse Way*. New York: Pantheon Books, 1975. Print.

Weiner, Harold F. *Tangled Up in Tunes: Ballad of a Dylanhead*. New York: Pencil Hill, 2012. Print.

White, E. B. "The Second Tree from the Corner." *55 Short Stories from the New Yorker*. New York: Simon and Schuster, 1965. 124–28. Print.

Wilder, Caryn. Letter to the David Gaines. July 27, 2013. Typescript.

Williams, Barry. *My Bob Dylan Story . . .!* Web. http://www.mybobdylanstory.com. June 10, 2013.

Williams, Paul. *Bob Dylan: Watching the River Flow, Observations on His Art-in-*

Progress 1966–1995. London: Omnibus, 1996. Print.

Williams, Richard. *Dylan: A Man Called Alias*. New York: Henry Holt and Company, 1992. Print.

Williamson, Nigel. *The Rough Guide to Bob Dylan*, 2nd ed. London: Penguin Books, 2006. Print.

Willis, Ellen. *Out of the Vinyl Deeps: Ellen Willis on Rock Music*. Minneapolis: U of Minnesota P, 2011. Print.

Wilson, Carl. *"Let's Talk About Love": A Journey to the End of Taste*. New York: Continuum International, 2007. Print.

Yaffe, David. *Bob Dylan: Like a Complete Unknown*. New Haven: Yale U, 2011. Print.

———. "Tangled Up in Bob." *The Nation* Apr. 25, 2005: 25–29. Print.

Young, Skip Dine. *Psychology at the Movies*. Hoboken, NJ: Wiley-Blackwell, 2011. Print.

CREDITS

Grateful thanks is given for permission to reprint lyrics from the following songs by Bob Dylan:

The following individuals have generously given me written permission to quote from either our conversations or our correspondence: Virginia Carwell, Don Dass, Mark Duffett, Phil Fitzpatrick, Babe Glumack, Bob Hocking, C. E. Holmes, Jamie Kallestad, Mary Keyes, Tony Petersen, and Caryn Wilder.

Barry Williams permitted me to quote from his tremendously helpful website about Dylan fans. Kelley Shaw consented to share her insightful words about Dylan and prophecy.

I again thank all concerned more than I can say.

INDEX

OF RELATED INTEREST